# TEACHING TO TRANSFORM URBAN SCHOOLS AND COMMUNITIES

For preservice candidates and novice teachers facing the challenges of feeling underprepared to teach in urban schools, this book offers a framework for conceptualizing, planning, and engaging in powerful teaching. Veteran teacher educator Etta R. Hollins builds on previous work to focus on transformative practices that emphasize the purpose and process of teaching. These practices are designed to improve academic performance, transform the social context in low-performing urban schools, and improve the quality of life in the local community.

The learning experiences provided in this book guide readers through a sequence of experiences for learning about the local community that include an examination of history and demographics, community resources, local city and federal governance structures, and collaborating with other professionals. Focus Questions and a dedicated Application to Practice section in each chapter further guide learning and help make real-world connections. Designed to enable readers to bridge the gaps between theory and practice and the actual needs of urban students and their communities, this groundbreaking text helps prepare preservice candidates to make a successful transition and aids novice teachers in developing teaching practices that support academic excellence.

**Etta R. Hollins** holds the Ewing Marion Kaufmann Endowed Chair for Urban Teacher Education at the University of Missouri-Kansas City, USA.

# TEACHING TO TRANSFORM URBAN SCHOOLS AND COMMUNITIES

Powerful Pedagogy in Practice

*Etta R. Hollins*

Routledge
Taylor & Francis Group

NEW YORK AND LONDON

First published 2019
by Routledge
52 Vanderbilt Avenue, New York, NY 10017

and by Routledge
2 Park Square, Milton Park, Abingdon, Oxon, OX14 4RN

*Routledge is an imprint of the Taylor & Francis Group, an informa business*

© 2019 Etta R. Hollins

*Library of Congress Cataloging-in-Publication Data*
A catalog record has been requested for this book

ISBN: 978-0-415-39913-5 (hbk)
ISBN: 978-1-138-71433-5 (pbk)
ISBN: 978-1-315-23083-2 (ebk)

Typeset in Bembo
by Swales & Willis Ltd, Exeter, Devon, UK

This book is dedicated to the young people whose lives are influenced in the present and in the future by the educational policies and practices in classrooms and schools.

# CONTENTS

# CONTRIBUTORS

**Curtis W. Branch** is a clinical psychologist in private practice in Hackensack, New Jersey.

**Etta R. Hollins** holds the Ewing Marion Kaufmann Endowed Chair for Urban Teacher Education at the University of Missouri-Kansas City, USA.

# PREFACE

This book addresses the well-documented challenge of candidates completing teacher preparation programs and becoming novice teachers while feeling under-prepared for teaching in urban schools. The practices in this book support candidates in making a successful transition to teaching in urban schools and help novice teachers develop a grounded approach to teaching practices. A twofold approach for accomplishing the intended outcome is presented. The first part of the conceptual framework for teaching includes a philosophical stance (purpose for teaching), a theoretical perspective on learning, a teaching process, and epistemic practices. The second part of the framework presents a process for supporting urban students' learning by embedding subject matter and skills in cultural knowledge and heritage, using familiar language and everyday experiences, helping students feel comfortable and supported in the classroom context, and understanding and developing a context and pedagogy responsive to students' life conditions.

The approach used in this book supports candidates and novice teachers in personalizing their practice by developing a philosophical stance focused on a well-thought-out statement of purpose for teaching that addresses the value of the subject matter being taught, the social context for learning, and the intended impact on the learner, the local community, and the larger society. When developing a personal stance, candidates are encouraged to consider the potential impact of different philosophical positions described by colleagues and in the scholarly literature. This helps in examining the value perspectives in a philosophical stance. The author does not recommend a specific philosophical stance.

Similarly, the author does not recommend a specific theoretical perspective. However, the theoretical perspective associated with teaching and textbooks in specific disciplines are presented. For example, mathematics and science textbooks use a constructivist theoretical perspective on learning, whereas history and social studies use a sociocultural theoretical perspective. The emphasis in this book is on the primacy of a theoretical perspective in understanding, evaluating and planning effective learning experiences, and knowing how to make adjustments that increase effectiveness for diverse learners.

Many texts on teaching underserved students focus on developing students' awareness of their position in society, promoting the desire to bring about social change, and providing opportunities for meaningful and productive learning. The present text promotes both social justice pedagogy and socially just pedagogy, but differs from other approaches in that it is focused on *transformative* practices that emphasize the purpose and process of teaching to ensure that every student reaches her or his highest potential, transform the academic and social context in low-performing urban schools, and improve the quality of life in the local community.

The discussion in this book guides candidates and novice teachers in developing deep knowledge of students through understanding child and adolescent growth and development, the personal experiences and life challenges students face within and outside of school, and the cultural and community context in which students are socialized. Understanding child and adolescent growth and development is contextualized within a racialized society and school context that influence personal identity, self-esteem, peer relationships, and emotional and psychological well-being. Deep knowledge of students includes understanding their life conditions, such as poverty, homelessness, foster care, court affiliation, and immigrant or refugee status. Many students face life challenges, such as depression, trauma, post-traumatic stress disorder, and toxic stress, that interfere with their ability to focus and learn from classroom instruction and that contribute to displaying unacceptable behaviors. The discussion in this book provides guidance and tools for candidates and novice teachers in collecting data on students' development and personal experiences for use in planning powerful learning experiences and supporting collaboration with medical and mental health professionals when appropriate.

An important part of child and adolescent development and students' experiential background is the cultural and community context in which they are socialized. The discussion in this book provides guidance for incorporating students' culture, heritage, and experiences into the curriculum and pedagogical practices. Understanding the local community as context and text for studying specific subject matter is based on knowledge about the local community that includes an examination of history and demographics, community resources, and local, state, and federal governance structures.

This book is organized into six chapters based on a conceptualization of teaching as an interpretive and transformative process and practice. Collectively, these chapters address the present conditions in urban schools, developing a purpose and approach for teaching that addresses the best interest of children and the community in which they live, employing powerful pedagogy grounded in deep knowledge of students, promoting solidarity and unity among students through academic and social competence, and teaching to restore wholeness for children living with adversity. The discussion in this book presents a transformative approach to the curriculum and pedagogy intended to ensure that every child reaches her or his highest potential and contributes to improving life conditions in the local community in the present and the future.

Chapter 1, "Teaching in the Shadow," is introspective for the teaching profession in examining a traditional approach to planning and enacting learning experiences and a social context in classrooms and schools that is inconsistent in supporting students' growth and development. In traditional approaches to school and classroom practices, some students receive greater benefit than others. This chapter is focused on examining the outcomes, practices, and policies in urban schools that contribute to such disparities, and that are often disconnected from the life experiences and needs of the students and the communities in which students live. This chapter presents evidence that this disconnection among school practices and students' life experiences contributes to present conditions in urban schools, including the wide variation in learning outcomes, the social context in schools, disparities in college and career readiness, and certain teaching quality indicators. Additionally, the discussion in this chapter addresses the relationship among the performance of local urban schools, household income, and the quality of life in the local community.

Chapter 2, "Teaching with Purpose," presents the first part of the conceptual framework for teaching to transform urban schools and communities. This chapter presents a scaffold for thinking about and planning meaningful and productive learning experiences, and for creating a comfortable and supportive context for learning. This approach to *teaching with purpose* includes the intentionally planned use of a philosophical stance, theoretical perspective, meaningfully framed curriculum, and thoughtfully designed pedagogy to serve the best interest of the learner and the community in which the learner lives. Teaching with purpose takes into consideration the present conditions and needs of the students, families, the local community, and the nation in framing the academic and other developmental goals for students.

Chapter 3, "Teaching from the Center," situates knowledge and standards from the grade level expectations, curriculum frameworks, or core curriculum within the cultural knowledge, heritage, cognition, language, literacy, and everyday experiences of the learner. This discussion includes understanding the local community as a resource for teaching from the center. Additionally, this discussion addresses ways to use as context and text the history, traditions, and accomplishments of specific groups when teaching subject matter, concepts, principles, and skills.

Chapter 4, "Teaching for Unity," is in the second part of the conceptual framework. Teaching for unity includes: (a) developing for each student a sense of belongingness, connectedness, and clarity of identity; (b) promoting attitudes of respect and inclusion among all students; (c) providing opportunities for collaborative learning experiences to ensure that each student meets the expected learning outcomes; and (d) promoting intergenerational connectedness. This chapter addresses the importance of teaching for unity in developing a spirit of teamwork and collective responsibility that, when combined with intergenerational connectedness, supports a commitment to maintaining and improving the local community. These aspects of unity are elaborated and examples are included.

Chapter 5, "Teaching to Restore," is focused on restoring the academic, psychological, and social well-being of children and youth who have experienced adversity, including trauma or toxic stress through abandonment, alienation, displacement, or neglect. The discussion addresses approaches to classroom support for students living with distracted parents, in poverty, homeless, in extended families, in foster care, group homes, incarcerated, and those who are immigrants or refugees.

Chapter 6, "Collaborating with Other Professionals," is focused on issues of emotional and mental health that are often omitted in teacher preparation programs, such as childhood depression, post-traumatic stress disorder (PTSD), trauma, toxic stress, and gang affiliation. The discussion in this chapter presents new data from clinical research that can be used by teachers in identifying children in need of professional evaluation, further assistance with emotional or behavioral disorders, and developing pedagogical practices to support children's growth and development during and after experiencing life-altering conditions or events.

Finally, this book builds upon and extends the discussion in my book *Culture in School Learning*, and can be used independently or as a companion. *Culture in School Learning* presents a basic framework for understanding the relationship among culture, cognition, and school learning. The application of this framework is situated within the conceptualization of teaching as an interpretive process and practice. *Teaching to Transform Urban Schools and Communities* builds upon and extends the basic tenets in *Culture in School Learning* to present a conceptualization of teaching that is both interpretive and transformative. In *Teaching to Transform Urban Schools and Communities*, the emphasis on developing a deep understanding of students includes child and adolescent growth and development within the context of a racialized society, students' culture and personal experiences within and outside of school, and the community context in which students live and are socialized. This knowledge is used in creating powerful pedagogy that supports students in identifying and developing the academic, social, and emotional skills, competency, and resources needed in their everyday lives in the present and the future, within and outside of school.

# 1

# TEACHING IN THE SHADOW

## Focus Questions

1. What accounts for the wide variations across states, school districts, schools, and individual teachers in the academic performance of traditionally underserved students?
2. How does the quality of schooling students receive in P-12 schools impact their quality of life as adults?

## Introduction

*Teaching in the shadow* is a traditional approach to planning and enacting learning experiences and a social context in classrooms and schools that does not consistently benefit or fit the needs of students in attendance at the school. In this approach to school and classroom practices, some students are consistently more successful and others are less so. Those teaching in the shadow may not fully understand the relationship among pedagogy, subject matter, learner characteristics, learning, and learning outcomes—and that teachers are responsible for planning productive learning experiences based on an understanding of this dynamic relationship. Further, teaching in the shadow employs naive classroom practices not well-suited to the school context; without full knowledge of the singular or collective impact of teachers on students' lives in the present, the future, and the intergenerational extension; and without knowledge of the wide variation in effectiveness and impact among teachers, schools, districts, and across states.

This chapter addresses the variations in outcomes, practices, and policies in urban schools that prepare students for success in life and uplift the community, or that contribute to disparities and are often disconnected from the life experiences and needs of the students and the communities in which students live. This chapter presents data and researched evidence that teaching in the shadow is one aspect of a reciprocal relationship among present practice, outcomes of schooling, and the conditions in urban communities. School practices contribute to the wide variation in learning outcomes across schools and teachers serving students in schools with similar characteristics, level of preparation for college and career readiness, social context in schools, and certain teaching quality indicators. The discussion in this chapter addresses the relationship among the performance of local urban schools, household income, and quality of life in the local community. Examples of the wide variation in the quality of education and learning outcomes based on race, ethnicity, and social class status across the nation in schools, school districts, and states are included in this discussion.

## Variation in School Outcomes for Underserved Students

There is wide variation in school practitioners' effectiveness with children and youth from urban and low-income communities. Across the nation, there are many high-performing, high-poverty, high-minority schools with a comfortable and supportive social context; however, this is not true for the majority of schools serving this population. Multiple reliable sources have documented variations in the academic performance of students attending urban schools, including the Nation's Report Card (NAEP) on the five megastates (California, Florida, Illinois, New York, and Texas), the NAEP Trial Urban School District Assessment (TUDA), the Broad Foundation-sponsored Broad Prize for Urban Education, and the Education Trust in its Dispelling the Myth Award. Each of these sources show variations among schools, school districts, and states serving populations with similar demographic characteristics. Many schools serving low-income minority students are high-performing; however, the majority of schools serving this demographic are low-performing. These data dispel many myths about school failure and raise new questions about policies and practices in classrooms and schools across education providers.

### *Variation in School Outcomes across States*

The Nation's Report Card on the five megastates (California, Florida, Illinois, New York, and Texas) provides important insights about variations in the academic performance across states (http://nationsreportcard.gov/megastates). These five states enroll almost 40% of the nation's public school students, serve half of the nation's English language learners, and include some of the highest concentrations of low-income students. Among the five megastates, California has the largest total student enrollment in public schools (6,289,578), the largest number of English language learners (1,467,989), and the highest student to teacher ratio (24.1). Florida has the highest percentage of students on free and reduced-price lunch (56%).

An update on the megastates using the NAEP 2015 results for Black students, including nine other states, illustrates the variation in student performance across states (National Center for Education Statistics, 2015). Each state included in this comparison has 50% or more of students eligible to receive free and reduced-price lunch, except New Jersey, with 33%. The percentage of Black students performing at or above proficient at eighth grade in mathematics was highest in New Jersey (20%) and lowest in Alabama (5%). In New Jersey, Black students were 14% of the total population tested at eighth grade in mathematics and 31% in Alabama (see Table 1.1). A similar analysis of reading shows that the percentage of Black students performing at or above proficient at eighth grade in reading was highest in New Jersey (24%) and lowest in Louisiana (10%). In New Jersey, Black students were 15% of the total population tested in reading at eighth grade and 44% in Louisiana (see Table 1.2). The megastates varied in the percentage of Black students in the population tested at eighth grade in mathematics and reading, and in the percentage of Black students performing at or above proficient. However, in the five megastates, Black students outperformed their Black peers in 7 of the 14 states in math and 6 of the 14 in reading.

Analyzing the performance of Black students across states is particularly informative because their performance is below that of most other students at each grade level and in the subject matter and skills areas tested by the NAEP. This variation across states in Black students' performance indicates that the students' life conditions may not be the most influential factor in their academic performance. For example, fluctuations in the poverty level or the percentage of Black students in the population do not correlate with their performance in

**TABLE 1.1** NAEP 2015 Black student performance in mathematics

| State | Black student enrollment | Percentage at or above basic | Percentage at or above proficient | Percentage at advanced |
|---|---|---|---|---|
| New Jersey | 14% | 60% | 20% | 4% |
| Texas* | 11% | 57% | 16% | 2% |
| North Carolina | 25% | 50% | 16% | 2% |
| New York* | 20% | 52% | 15% | 2% |
| California* | 7% | 45% | 14% | 1% |
| Illinois* | 16% | 49% | 12% | 1% |
| Florida* | 23% | 45% | 11% | 1% |
| Mississippi | 50% | 45% | 10% | 1% |
| Arkansas | 22% | 42% | 10% | 1% |
| Tennessee | 20% | 41% | 9% | 1% |
| Oklahoma | 9% | 47% | 8% | # |
| South Carolina | 34% | 42% | 8% | 1% |
| Louisiana | 47% | 39% | 7% | # |
| Alabama | 31% | 33% | 5% | # |

\* Megastates account for 40% of the total population of K-12 students in the United States.

**TABLE 1.2** NAEP 2015 Black student performance in reading

| State | Black student enrollment | Percentage at or above basic | Percentage at or above proficient | Percentage at advanced |
|---|---|---|---|---|
| New Jersey | 15% | 69% | 24% | 2% |
| Florida* | 21% | 65% | 20% | 1% |
| New York* | 17% | 61% | 20% | 1% |
| California* | 6% | 62% | 18% | 1% |
| North Carolina | 25% | 60% | 18% | 1% |
| Oklahoma | 8% | 59% | 15% | # |
| Illinois* | 15% | 56% | 15% | 1% |
| Texas* | 12% | 58% | 14% | # |
| Tennessee | 20% | 52% | 13% | # |
| South Carolina | 34% | 52% | 12% | # |
| Arkansas | 19% | 51% | 12% | # |
| Alabama | 31% | 49% | 12% | # |
| Mississippi | 49% | 50% | 11% | # |
| Louisiana | 44% | 51% | 10% | # |

* Megastates account for 40% of the total population of K-12 students in the United States.

mathematics and reading. One factor to consider is that each of the 50 states in the nation is responsible for public education, preschool through college and the education of teachers and administrators. Each state develops regulations, policies, and practices to govern and guide public education. Most states have policies supporting special instruction and accommodation for teaching English language learners and special needs students. The overrepresentation of Black students in special education for learning disabilities and emotional disturbance is common knowledge in the field. Research studies have identified several cognitive and linguistic accommodations and interventions that significantly improve Black students' academic performance (Brown & Ryoo, 2008; Lee, 1995; Moses, Kamii, Swap, & Howard 1989; Nasir, Hand, & Taylor, 2008; Tatum, 2005). However, these specific cognitive or linguistic accommodations for Black students are not evident in state policies. It is difficult to determine the extent to which differences in state policies and practices influence variations in learning outcomes among particular subgroups of students, although it is a salient issue for investigation. Further, this analysis raises questions about the role of curriculum, school policies, and teaching practices.

### Variation across School Districts

In 2017, 27 school districts participated in the NAEP Trial Urban School District Assessment (TUDA). The percentage of students performing at or above proficient in mathematics and reading in TUDA school districts varied widely. A few TUDA school districts met or exceeded national percentages. Nationally, 34% of all students performed at or above proficient in mathematics at eighth grade, and 36% in reading. Among the 27 TUDA school districts, three met or exceeded the national percentage, performing at or above proficient in mathematics at eighth grade (San Diego, 36%; Austin, 38%; and Charlotte, 41%). In reading, at eighth grade, one TUDA school district met the national percentage (Austin, 36%). Austin met or exceeded national percentages in both mathematics and reading at eighth grade.

Further analysis of the NAEP Trial Urban School District Assessment data revealed within-state differences across districts in the academic performance of Black and Hispanic students in mathematics and reading at eighth grade. Nationally, 18% of Black students and 23% of Hispanic students performed at or above proficient in reading at eighth grade. For example, among the four TUDA districts in Texas (Austin, Dallas, Fort Worth, and Houston), in reading at eighth grade only Hispanic students in Austin met the national percentage. Black students performed six or more points below the national percentage in all four districts, and Hispanic students performed seven or more points below the national percentage in three of the four districts. The three TUDA districts in Florida (Duval County, Hillsborough County, and Miami-Dade) exceeded the national percentage, performing at or above proficient in reading at eighth grade for Hispanic students by five or more points, and Black students performed at the national percentage for one district and one or two points below the national percentage in two of the three districts. These variations in academic performance across school districts serving populations of students with similar characteristics raise important questions about the quality of schooling provided, and differences in policies and practices.

## Variation across Schools

Since 2003, the Education Trust has selected high-performing, high-poverty, high-minority schools for its Dispelling the Myth Award. The schools selected for this award have achieved results at or near the top in the state across grades and subject areas for several years and are not selective in admission. Most awards go to regular neighborhood schools with a designated attendance area, but a few awards are to schools that hold blind lotteries for admission. Elementary, middle and high schools are eligible for this award. The profiles for schools receiving the Dispelling the Myth Award are on the Education Trust website at https://edtrust.org/dispelling_the_myth/.

North Godwin Elementary School in Grand Rapids, Michigan was first recognized with the Dispelling the Myth Award in 2009 and revisited in 2013. In 2013, the total enrollment at North Godwin Elementary School was 417 students, with 22% African American, 38% Latino, 36% White, 4% Asian, and

75% low-income. This school has continued to meet and exceed state standards, with 84% of fourth-graders meeting reading standards in comparison to the state average of 68% and 74% of fourth-graders meeting state standards compared to 45% statewide.

Roxbury Preparatory Charter School in Roxbury, Massachusetts received the Dispelling the Myth Award in 2008. This middle school enrolls 198 students admitted by lottery. The student enrollment includes 61% African American, 33% Latino, 4% two or more races, 2% Native American, 30% English language learners, and 70% low-income. The students at Roxbury Preparatory Charter School perform well above statewide percentages in meeting state standards in English language arts and math. In English language arts in 2008, 90% of Roxbury students met state standards as compared to 74% statewide. In math, 86% of Roxbury students met state standards as compared to 49% statewide. Additionally, 60% of the graduates attended or graduated from college.

Jack Britt High School in Fayetteville, North Carolina received the Dispelling the Myth Award in 2010. This high school has an enrollment of 2,000 students that includes 46% White, 39% African American, 10% Latino, 4% Asian, 1% Native American, and 25% low-income. Jack Britt High School graduated more than 90% of it students as compared to 80% statewide. This school has a higher pass rate on state-mandated tests than most other high schools in the state. On the state-mandated algebra test, 93% of Jack Britt students passed, including 91% of African American students, compared to 79% statewide for all students and 55% for African American students statewide.

The extent to which the specific practices in high-performing urban schools, when identified and successfully replicated, will transform low-performing urban schools has not been determined. Hollins (2012) reported a study that employed a *structured dialogue* approach to transform teaching practices and improve student learning outcomes in kindergarten through fourth grade in a low-performing urban school. The findings from this study indicated that when teachers developed an understanding of the relationship among teaching practices, learner characteristics, and learning outcomes, they were able to make adjustments in their teaching practices to improve learning outcomes for their students. Once teachers understood how to adjust their pedagogy to improve learning outcomes, they took responsibility for student learning and took pride in their students' academic performance. The findings from this study indicate that teaching is the central factor in student academic performance.

## Quality Teaching as a Factor in School Outcomes

There is little doubt that the quality of teaching and access to high-quality learning experiences are at the heart of students' academic achievement and performance. The New Teacher Project (2013) has identified outstanding teachers for the Fishman Prize since 2012. Essays written by recipients of this award provide insights into their teaching practices and relationships with students. These teachers carefully plan instruction to accomplish specific learning outcomes based on students' learning needs, interests, values, prior knowledge, and experiences. Instruction consists of well-organized and clearly articulated approaches and routines. Students are actively engaged in meaningful and productive learning experiences. Teachers monitor student learning and provide prompt feedback and assistance as needed to support student learning and achieving learning outcomes. The recipients of the Fishman Prize were highly motivated, took responsibility for student learning, invested time and energy in planning and executing high-quality instruction, and regularly assessed student learning and instructional practices.

These examples of high-performing teachers reveal the power of individual teachers in classrooms and schools. An individual high-performing teacher makes a very important contribution to the lives of the students he or she teaches and can influence colleagues, even in a low-performing urban school. However, a community of high-performing teachers working together can directly transform academic performance and the social context in a low-performing school. High-performing schools depend on individual high-performing teachers. The discussion in the subsequent chapters in this book will support you in reaching your highest potential as a classroom teacher.

Increasing access to high-quality teaching and learning experiences is an important factor influencing learning outcomes and for improving low-performing schools. High school graduation rates, high school dropout rates, and school attendance (including suspension and expulsion) are important indicators of the quality of teaching and learning, as well as school effectiveness. This suggests that recruiting and retaining high-performing teachers is essential for improving low-performing schools. The New Teacher Project (2012) reported that high-performing and low-performing teachers leave large urban school districts at approximately the same rate. These researchers estimated that approximately 10,000 high-performing teachers leave the 50 largest school districts each year, while 100,000 low-performing teachers remain. The result is that first-year beginning teachers are more effective than 40% of the experienced teachers in the largest school districts.

Further, the findings from the New Teacher Project (2012) study show that principals encouraged low-performing and high-performing teachers to stay at the school at about the same rate. Interviews with low-performing teachers revealed that they viewed themselves as above-average in their performance. High-performing teachers were discouraged by a lack of support and encouragement from principals at their schools. High-performing teachers wanted feedback and professional development, recognition, more responsibility, advancement, and resources to support their work in the classroom. Low-performing teachers often received more responsibility and advancement than high-performing colleagues.

The impact of low-performing teachers on the academic performance of students and the social context is evident in low-performing schools. Sipe (2004), a first-year teaching fellow who completed a three-month alternative teacher certification program, described his experience in failing middle school in New York City. Sipe described the condition of the school building as in serious disrepair, similar to a dangerous subway, and with a prison-like environment. The relationship between teachers and students, as well as among peers, was one of conflict and hostility. Sipe (2004) described his experience in the following reflection:

> I remember being repulsed by colleagues who referred to their students as "bitches," "assholes," and "animals," to name but a few epithets. But given the oppositional atmosphere of our school, this same dehumanization strategy is perhaps a natural, if extremely distressing, reaction to the circumstances: If a disruptive student insults you what does it matter? After all, he or she is just an "asshole." And if your students do not learn, well, it is because they are "animals." This logic does not make the place any more pleasant and it wreaks havoc on the educational mission, but for some it makes the job more bearable.
>
> *(p. 333)*

Sipe did not describe his own teaching practices or those of his colleagues. However, he seems to be empathetic with colleagues in their interaction with students and their decision to leave the school. Sipe decided to leave the school at the end of his first year of teaching.

Hemmings (2003) investigated the social context in two urban high schools by documenting the experiences and perceptions of six seniors through observations and conversations. At both high schools, disharmony, conflict, and confrontations characterized relationships between teachers and students and among students. Hemmings described the conflict and confrontations in the classroom and corridors as a struggle for respect, which relates to power and authority. Hemmings (2003) argued:

> Both teachers and students in the exercise of authority owe allegiance to a moral order that supports good teaching and genuine learning. The model works smoothly when the moral order forges trust between competent teachers and their students. Trouble occurs, and a crisis of authority arises, when the moral order is unsettled or broken down.
>
> *(p. 417)*

Hemmings (2003) described the practices of teachers whose classrooms were chaotic. In these classrooms, the purpose of the subject matter lacked clarity, learning experiences were not meaningful or clearly articulated, and students perceived teachers as not caring about them. The students believed that their disrespect for these teachers was justified based on the quality of the instruction they received. In essence, the students felt disrespected by the teachers. Students respected teachers in classrooms where the purpose for the subject matter was well-understood, learning experiences were clearly articulated and meaningful, and teachers provided assistance and support as needed. The students felt that these teachers deserved respect because of the quality of instruction provided and that the teachers cared about students and their future. The description of effective teachers in Hemmings' (2003) study is similar to that in the New Teacher Project (2012) study.

State interventions in schools and school districts aimed at improving learning outcomes take a broader approach that includes leadership, use of data to guide classroom instruction, and a positive school climate. Klute, Cherasaro, and Apthrop (2016) conducted a review of studies focused on the relationship between state intervention in chronically failing schools and student achievement. These authors identified 122 specific interventions spread across five categories that included turnaround schools with partners, school improvement planning with additional funding, school restructuring, changes in the entity operating the school, and school closure. The results in each category were mixed across schools and states. In some schools, state intervention resulted in improvement in student achievement and in others it did not. Some researchers attributed school improvement to strong leadership, use of data to guide instruction, positive school culture characterized by trust, and increased expectations for students. Klute et al. (2016) reported that:

> A substantial limitation in the existing literature is that most studies used a research design that does not permit causal conclusions about the effects of these interventions. Less than a third of identified studies used a quasi-experimental design that compared schools that received an intervention to schools that did not . . . Many of these studies had serious limitations, including confounds created when only one school was assigned to each condition or when the treatment and control groups attended school at widely different points in time. Other studies did not provide the information needed to assess the extent to which treatment and comparison groups were similar at the start of intervention.
>
> *(p. 10)*

Inconsistencies in the quality of research on school improvement leave many unanswered questions about opportunities for successful replication of practices in high-performing schools and school districts.

## Other Indicators of School Quality

The previous discussion focused on academic performance as an important indicator of school quality. High school graduation rate is another indicator of the quality of schooling provided for the nation's youth (Figure 1.1). In 2014, the nation achieved the historical high school graduation rate of 82.3% for

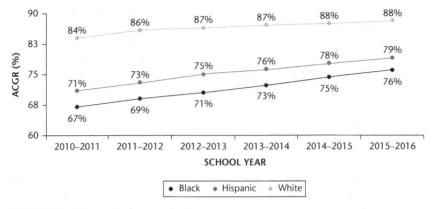

**FIGURE 1.1** Adjusted cohort graduation rate

the entering ninth grade cohort. However, the high school graduation rate was significantly lower for underserved students (African American, 72.5%; Hispanic, 76.3%; and low-income, 74.6%). In 2014, there were 1,009 high schools across the nation with a graduation rate of 67% or less. These high schools served 924,918 students that included high percentages of traditionally underserved students (Black, 36.09%; Hispanic, 26.63%; and low-income, 65.36%) (*Building a Grad Nation*, 2018). These data show the discrepancy in educational outcomes by ethnicity and race.

In addition to low academic performance and a low high school graduation rate, many low-performing schools serving urban and low-income students are characterized by conflict, dissension, strife, and a struggle for power and respect between teachers and students and among students. This type of contextual discord often results from an imbalance in school policies and practices related to developing a positive and supportive social context for learning. In these low-performing, high-conflict situations, administrators and teachers tend to focus more attention on constraints, boundaries, and consequences rather than guidance, support, affordances, and opportunities. The result is a reliance on suspensions, expulsions, and referral to law enforcement for maintaining control and order in schools. Suspensions and expulsions often begin in preschool.

Based on a report from the U.S. Department of Education Office for Civil Rights (2014), in the 2011–2012 school year, 49 million students were enrolled in the nation's elementary and secondary schools, 3.5 million students received in-school suspensions, 1.9 million students received out-of-school suspensions, 1.55 million students received multiple out-of-school suspensions, and 130,000 students were expelled from school. School suspensions, expulsions, and school-related contact with law enforcement disproportionately ensnared traditionally underserved students. For example, 20% of African American boys and 12% of African American girls received out-of-school suspensions as compared to 6% of

White boys and 2% of White girls. Similarly, African American students represented 16% of school enrollment, but 27% of students referred to law enforcement and 31% of school-related arrests, as compared to White students, who represented 51% of school enrollment, but 41% of referrals to law enforcement and 39% of school-related arrests. School discipline involving suspensions, expulsions, referrals to law enforcement, and school-related arrests tend to be more frequent in low-performing urban schools than in schools with better student learning outcomes.

School suspensions, expulsions, and school-related arrests are part of the school-to-prison pipeline. Many students referred by schools to law-enforcement are arrested and receive criminal records for minor offenses such as disrupting class, disorderly conduct, inappropriate language, defiance, and violating the dress code. According to a report by the American Bar Association Joint Task Force on Reversing the School-to-Prison Pipeline, "on any given day some 20,000 young people are in juvenile detention centers; 54,000 in youth prisons or other confinement; 4,200 in adult jails; and 1,200 in adult prisons" (Redfield & Nance, 2016, p. 42). Most of these young people (87%) were incarcerated for nonviolent offenses and 66% were youth of color. The recidivism rate among incarcerated youth is high, often leading to imprisonment in adulthood. These harsh discipline practices in schools have a long-term negative impact on urban communities by increasing the probability for crime, violence, unemployment, poverty, and single-parent families.

## The Impact of School Quality on Communities

The quality of education and the social context in schools serving urban and low-income students have a *measurable* impact on the quality of life for local residents, including employment, household income, access to healthcare, social and emotional well-being, values, and perceptions. The quality and extent of one's education influences the ability to manage everyday frustrations, solve problems, and avoid negative encounters with law enforcement. Receiving a poor quality of academic preparation in elementary and secondary schools increases the probability for high school dropouts and decreases access to higher education. Further, a negative social context in schools increases the propensity for conflict and violence in urban communities in situations where the student peer culture emerges as the primary mechanism for socialization and preparation for adult life. Without appropriate adult guidance in schools, peers easily socialize students into illicit activities, including early sex, drugs, and gangs.

### Educational Attainment and Income

The relationship between education, employment, and household income is well-documented. Educational attainment is uneven across subpopulations in the United States. One example of disproportionate distribution of educational attainment is the percentages of subpopulations with a bachelor's degree (White, 36%; Black,

22%; Hispanic, 15%) (Ryan & Bauman, 2016). According to the U.S. Census Bureau, in 2015 in the United States, approximately 13.5% of the total population (43.1 million people) lived in poverty or below the federal poverty level (Proctor, Semega, & Kollar, 2016). Those living below the federal poverty level include individuals with an annual income less than $12,000 and a family of three earning $20,000 or less. Particular ethnic groups are disproportionately represented among those living below the federal poverty level (White, 11.6%; Hispanic, 21.4%; Black, 24.1%). A higher percentage of individuals with less education live in poverty than their peers with more education (no high school diploma, 26.3%; high school diploma, 12.9%; some college, 9.6%; bachelor's degree, 4.5%). In 2015, a higher percentage of individuals with less education were unemployed than their peers with more education (no high school diploma, 8.0%; high school diploma, 5.4%; some college, 5.0%; bachelor's degree, 2.8%). These data clearly demonstrate the relationship between educational attainment, household income, and unemployment (Figure 1.2). Further, these data show disparities among subpopulations in each of these areas as reported by the Census Bureau.

Educational attainment is an apparent central factor in the quality of life for every citizen of the United States. The quality and opportunities for learning and the social context in low-performing urban schools have a long-term negative impact on students as individuals and on the communities in which they live. The limited opportunities for learning, referrals to law enforcement, and school-related arrests increase the probability for illiteracy, unemployment, low-income, and incarceration. Some scholars and practitioners argue that there is at least a reciprocal relationship between the social context in low-performing schools and violence in the local community. In a report sponsored by the U.S. Department of Justice's Office of Juvenile Justice and Delinquency Prevention (2016), it was pointed out that:

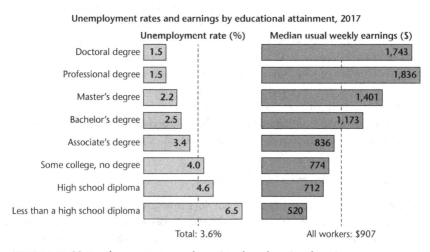

**FIGURE 1.2** Unemployment rates and earnings by educational attainment

Too many children in the United States are growing up in homes and communities where they witness or experience violence. Repeated exposure to violence and subsequent trauma can impact a young person's health, ability to succeed in school, their likelihood of becoming a victim or perpetrator of violence, and overall, their opportunity to stay on the right track.

However, an important function of schooling is to replace ignorance and inappropriate behavior with new academic and social knowledge and skills. When this important function fails, and the social context in schools warrants suspension, expulsion, and school-related arrests, the local community is directly impacted.

The school-to-prison pipeline contributes to the process of mass incarceration. According the U.S. Department of Justice, "At yearend 2015, an estimated 2,173,800 persons were either under the jurisdiction of state or federal prisons or in the custody of local jails in the United States, down about 51,300 persons compared to yearend 2014" (Kaeble & Glaze, 2016, p. 2). The composition of the prison population is similar to the population of students who experience school-related arrests in that both are disproportionately people of color, low-income, and undereducated. At year end 2015, there were 693,300 inmates confined in local jails—48.3% White, 35.1% Black, Hispanic 14.3%. According to a report from the Executive Office of the President of the United States (2016), interaction with the criminal justice system, including arrests and incarceration, are disproportionately concentrated among African Americans, Hispanics, the poor, and individuals with mental illness and substance abuse. Similarly, African Americans, Hispanics, and the poor are disproportionately represented in school referrals to law enforcement and school-related arrests. It is further pointed out that:

> In addition to its direct costs, the criminal justice system also imposes substantial collateral consequences on individuals with criminal records, their families and communities. Having a criminal record makes it more difficult to find employment and depresses earnings. Criminal sanctions can also have negative consequences for individuals' health, debt, transportation, housing, and food security. These consequences add up to large and lasting negative impacts for incarcerated individuals' families and communities.
> *(Executive Office of the President of the United States, 2016, p. 8)*

Many social and political factors contribute to mass incarceration; however, the significance of the contribution of schools and school practitioners is undeniable. The majority of inmates over 18 years of age did not graduate from high school and most have low level literacy skills. Failure to achieve grade level proficiency in literacy by third grade is a well-known predictor for dropping out of high school. Students who do not achieve proficiency in early literacy are prone to struggle with completing assignments for subject area courses in high school. The long-term persistent daily failure in school easily reaches a level of toxic stress. Toxic stress increases the likelihood for misbehavior and violation of school rules. School administrators often respond to students' misbehavior and minor violations of school rules with harsh punishment rather than addressing the core problems of academic and social competence. When the harsh punishment includes referrals to law enforcement and school-related arrests, school officials have initiated the process of incarceration for students.

### Educational Attainment and Health

Additionally, the quality and extent of education students receive will impact their health and longevity. According to the Robert Wood Johnson Foundation (2009), educational attainment is linked to health in three ways: "health knowledge and behaviors; employment and income; and social and psychological factors, including sense of control, social standing and social support" (p. 1). Typically, a higher level of educational attainment contributes to a longer and healthier life. Further, the effects of educational attainment are intergenerational. Children born to college-educated parents tend to be healthier and have higher levels of academic achievement in school than those whose parents did not complete high school.

In an analysis of the relationship between education and health, Feinstein, Sabates, Anderson, Sorhaindo, and Hammond (2006) pointed out that students learn from both the context in schools and the explicit curriculum and pedagogy. In school, students learn how to relate to peers and adults. This socialization often occurs through an unguided peer culture. The social interaction among students and between students and teachers influences students' development, including personal and social identity formation, group membership, self-confidence, and self-esteem. Each of these social and psychological factors influences students' mental health, physical health, and social relationships as adults. The curriculum and pedagogy support the development of subject matter knowledge, academic and cognitive skills, and personal values. The social context and the school curriculum and pedagogy have an impact on the educational attainment, health, and future income of students.

## Application to Practice

Application to practice of the information presented in this chapter requires that administrators and teachers take responsibility for transforming urban schools to have a positive impact on urban communities. Transforming urban schools means rethinking teaching practices and school policies to ensure that every student develops the competencies and skills necessary for success in school and life. The information in this chapter points to the importance of making observations and compiling data on the academic, psychological, and social development of students in school; high school graduation rate, college attendance/completion, and career preparation; and employment, income range, and contributions to the community. Transforming urban schools requires using the observations and data collected for identifying and addressing areas of school policies and practices in need of improvement.

Variations in the underperformance of Black and Hispanic students across states, school districts, and schools indicate that the problem is more likely to be located in school policies and teaching practices than in the characteristics and experiences of the students. The disparities among students in academic performance indicate that existing practices are more effective in supporting learning for some students than for others. The data call for carefully examining the relationship among theories of learning, student characteristics, curriculum content and framing, pedagogical practices, and learning outcomes.

The conflicts and power struggles between teachers and students and among students, as well as high rates of suspension, expulsion, referral to law enforcement, and school-related arrests, indicate the need for including social skills development in the curriculum and for training teachers in techniques for relationship-building. The evidence from data on harsh discipline shows that these practices do not teach students the social skills they need and they do not improve the social context in urban schools.

## Chapter Summary

*Teaching in the shadow* is a traditional approach to planning and enacting learning experiences and a social context in classrooms and schools that does not consistently benefit or fit the needs of the students in attendance at the school. In this approach to school and classroom practices, some students are consistently more successful and others are less so. The evidence presented in this chapter reveals important facts about students' academic performance, the social context in urban schools, the impact of schools on urban communities, and the responsibilities of administrators and teachers in urban schools. *Teaching in the shadow* is a naive practice that produces and supports the present disparities in academic performance among traditionally underserved students.

The discussion in this chapter revealed significant variation in the academic performance of Black and Hispanic students across states, school districts, and schools. In some urban schools and school districts, Black and Hispanic students outperformed their peers in other locations. Some teachers in low-performing schools foster high academic outcomes for their students, while their colleagues describe the same students as unmotivated, disengaged, and disrespectful. The fact that Black and Hispanic students are high-performing in some contexts and not others indicates that student characteristics such as income, neighborhood quality, and parents' education are not accurate predictors of students' ability to learn. Particular contextual factors within the school and classroom have greater accuracy in predicting students' academic performance. The evidence presented in this chapter supports the quality of teaching as a highly salient factor in students' learning outcomes.

Other indicators of school quality include high school graduation rate and discipline practices involving exclusion of students from classroom learning. The graduation rate in many urban high schools, and for underserved students, is well below the national average of 82% of the entering ninth grade cohort. The high school graduation rate is related to the performance in mathematics and reading at eighth grade. Another indicator of school quality is the rate of suspensions, expulsions, referrals to law enforcement, and school-related arrests. Data from the U.S. Department of Education indicate disproportionate administration of harsh punishment to Black and Hispanic students. Harsh discipline practices are fodder for school failure, juvenile detention, and adult incarceration.

Academic performance and other qualities of urban schools influence the quality of life in urban communities, including income, health, crime, and violence. Low-performing urban schools prepare students with low levels of skills in mathematics and reading. This limits their options for post-secondary education or occupational training. Many students educated in low-performing urban schools receive preparation suitable only for low-wage jobs and high rates of unemployment. Inadequate literacy and mathematics skills and inadequate financial resources limit access to proper healthcare for families impacted by low-performing urban schools. Harsh discipline practices in school often leads to anxiety, stress, increased resistance to authority, dropping out of school, juvenile detention, and adult incarceration. Adult incarceration disrupts family units, and increases homelessness and child placement in foster care. Unemployment and homelessness increase crime and violence in urban communities.

Applying to practice the knowledge presented in this chapter requires that administrators and teachers take responsibility for transforming urban schools to have a positive impact on urban communities. This means rethinking teaching practices and school policies to ensure that every student develops the competencies and skills necessary for success in school and life.

## References

Brown, B. A. & Ryoo, K. (2008). Teaching science as a language: A "content-first" approach to science teaching. *Journal of Research in Science Teaching*, 45(5), 529–553.

*Building a Grad Nation: Progress and challenges in raising high school graduation rates* (2018). Baltimore, MD: Civic Enterprises, Everyone Graduates Center at School of Education at Johns Hopkins University. Retrieved from http://gradnation.americaspromise.org/2018-building-grad-nation-report.

Chetty, R., Freidman, J., & Rockoff, J. (2014). Measuring the impact of teachers II: Teacher valued-added and student outcomes in adulthood. *American Economic Review*, 104(9), 2633–2679.

Executive Office of the President of the United States (2016). *Economic perspectives on incarceration and the criminal justice system*. Washington, DC: Author.

Feinstein, L., Sabates, R., Anderson, T. M., Sorhaindo, A., & Hammond, C. (2006). What are the effects of education on health? In *Measuring the effects of education on health and civic engagement: Proceedings of the Copenhagen symposium* (pp. 171–340).

Hemmings, A. (2003). Fighting for respect in urban high schools. *Teachers College Record*, 105(3), 416–437.

Hollins, E. R. (2012). *Learning to teach in urban schools*. New York: Routledge.

Kaeble, D. & Glaze, L. (2016). *Correctional populations in the United States, 2015*. Washington, DC: U.S. Department of Justice, Office of Justice Programs, Bureau of Justice Statistics.

Klute, M., Cherasaro, T., & Apthrop, H. (2016). *Summary of research on the association between state intervention in chronically low-performing schools and student achievement*. Washington, DC: National Center for Education Evaluation and Regional Assistance, Institute of Education Sciences, U.S. Department of Education.

Lee, C. D. (1995). A culturally based cognitive apprenticeship: Teaching African American high school students skills in literacy interpretation. *Reading Research Quarterly*, 30(4), 608–630.

Moses, R. P., Kamii, M., Swap, S. M., & Howard, J. (1989). The algebra project: Organizing in the spirit of Ella. *Harvard Educational Review*, 59(4), 423–443.

Nasir, N. S., Hand, V., & Taylor, E. V. (2008). Culture and mathematics in school: Boundaries between "culture" and "domain" knowledge in the mathematics classroom and beyond. *Review of Research in Education*, 32, 187–240.

National Center for Education Statistics (2015). *The Nation's Report Card: 2015 mathematics and reading assessment*. Washington, DC: National Center for Education Statistics, Institute of Education Sciences, U.S. Department of Education.

New Teacher Project (2012). *The irreplaceables: Understanding the real retention crisis in America's urban schools*. Retrieved from www.tntp.org.

New Teacher Project (2013). *The Fishman Prize series*. Retrieved from www.tntp.org/fishmanprize/2013.

Proctor, B. D., Semega, J. L., & Kollar, M. A. (2016, September). *Income and poverty in the United States: 2015*. U.S. Census Bureau, Current Population Reports, P60-256(RV). Washington, DC: U.S. Government Printing Office.

Redfield, S. E. & Nance, J. P. (2016). *School-to-Prison Pipeline: Defending Liberty Pursuing Justice*. Washington, DC: American Bar Association.

Robert Wood Johnson Foundation (2009). *Education matters for health*. Issue Brief 6: Education Health. Commission to Build a Healthier America. Princeton, NJ: Author.

Ryan, C. L. & Bauman, K. (2016, March). *Educational attainment in the United States: 2015*. U.S. Census Bureau, Current Population Reports. Washington, DC: U.S. Government Printing Office.

Sipe, R. (2004). Voices inside schools: Newjack—Teaching in a failing middle school. *Harvard Education Review*, 74(3), 330–339.

Tatum, A. W. (2005). *Teaching reading to Black adolescent males: Closing the achievement gap*. Portland, ME: Stenhouse Publishers.

U.S. Department of Education Office for Civil Rights (2014). *Civil rights data collection. Data snapshot: School discipline*. Washington, DC: Author.

U.S. Department of Justice, Office of Juvenile Justice and Delinquency Prevention (2016). *The Facts on Children's Exposure to Violence*. Retrieved from www.defendingchildhood.org.

Yen, I. H., Gregorich, S., Cohen, A. K., & Stewart, A. (2013). A community cohort study about childhood social and economic circumstances: Racial/ethnic differences and association with educational attainment and health of older adults. *BJM Open*, 3(4): e002140. doi:10.1136/bmjopen-2012-002140 PMCID: PMC3641446. bjm.com.

# 2

# TEACHING WITH PURPOSE

## Focus Questions

1. What is your purpose for teaching a specific subject or grade level? How will your students benefit now and in the future from what and how you teach?
2. What contribution will your teaching make to your students' communities and to the nation?
3. How will you develop coherence, continuity, and consistency in your teaching practice?

## Introduction

Every child and youth in the United States deserves opportunities to attend highly effective schools with caring and competent teachers, where the curriculum and pedagogy advance their academic knowledge and skills, and the context supports their emotional and social development. All children and youth deserve the opportunity to develop into well-educated adults with the capacity to provide adequate resources and support for themselves and their families, and to make a positive contribution to their communities and to the nation. Data presented in the previous chapter is evidence that access to high-quality public schools is possible for all students, including those traditionally underserved.

This chapter presents a conceptual model for *teaching with purpose*. This conceptual model supports thinking about and planning meaningful and productive learning experiences, and a comfortable and supportive social context for learning. The conceptual model for teaching with purpose encompasses five frames of practice that include the intentionally planned use of a philosophical stance, theoretical perspective, curriculum situated in context, epistemic practices, and

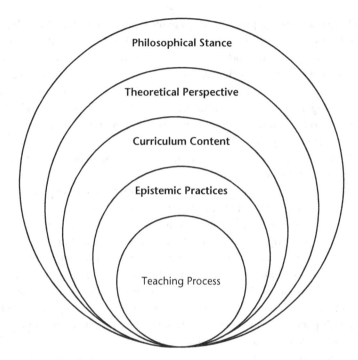

**FIGURE 2.1** Teaching with purpose conceptual model

a teaching process (Figure 2.1). Teaching with purpose takes into consideration the present conditions and needs of the students, families, the local community, and the nation in framing classroom learning. Teaching with purpose is an approach that prepares students to meet specific local needs, as well as to improve the general conditions and quality of life in the local community and nationally.

## Developing a Philosophical Stance

Teaching in P-12 schools is much more than facilitating students' learning of academic knowledge and skills. Teaching socializes students into the national core values, traditions, and ideological perspectives. Through engaging in classroom and school practices, youngsters learn moral and ethical perspectives and appropriate or accepted social norms. Students develop their personal and social identities, develop friendships, and begin finding their place in the world through the socialization process in classrooms and schools. Teaching is a complex process that supports students in reaching their greatest potential as individuals with the intellectual skills for ethical and responsible decision-making, as well as social and political participation in their local communities and the nation.

Teaching is a complex professional practice that requires deep knowledge of learning, learners, pedagogy, and subject matter. Additionally, effective teaching requires the integration and application of a well-thought-out philosophical stance that includes clearly articulated statements of the purpose for teaching, the value of knowledge and skills taught, a well-articulated conceptualization of the teaching process, and commitments and responsibilities. *Teaching with purpose* refers to the intentionally planned use of a theoretical perspective, curriculum, and pedagogy to serve the best interest of the learner, the community in which the learner lives, and the nation. This discussion presents an example of a philosophical stance.

A philosophical stance for teaching practice has four interdependent components that guide teaching and learning in classrooms. The first component is a *statement of the purpose* for teaching and its relationship to the nation and local community. This component situates classroom learning within the context of the needs and resources of the local community. The second component is a *statement of the value* and primary benefit of specific subject matter in the curriculum for individual students in the present and the future, and its contribution to the local community and to the larger society. This *value statement* supports providing students with personal connections to the subject matter. The third component is a *definition of teaching*, including the elements of teaching practice, and the individual and societal outcomes incorporated in the philosophical stance. The definition of teaching describes the relationship among teaching practice, learning outcomes, and societal impact. The fourth component is a *statement of personal commitments and responsibilities* for teaching. Each component of the philosophical stance is a clearly articulated perspective supported by research, theory, and data collected on students and the local community.

The codes of ethics for education associations describe the specific responsibilities for education practitioners related to children, students, families, colleagues, local communities and the nation, and professional competence. These professional codes of ethics present ethical and moral standards for the profession that serve as an important basic orientation for thinking about your own philosophical stance and purpose for teaching. Two examples of professional education codes of ethics are those developed by the National Association for the Education of Young Children (NAEYC) and the National Association of State Directors of Teacher Education and Certification (NASDTEC).

John Dewey's "My Pedagogic Creed" (1897), published in the *School Journal*, is an example of a philosophical stance that includes a definition of education, statement of the purpose of schooling, description of the subject matter of education, teaching approaches and methods, and the relationship between school and the social process. This philosophical stance is a complex explanation of the purpose and process of schooling, as well as its potential social impact. Carefully reading John Dewey's pedagogical creed will give you a good idea of how to begin developing your own philosophical stance based on what you know about school practices, learning theory, research, pedagogy, and the social conditions and needs of traditionally underserved students and their communities.

The philosophical stance framing the discussion in this book holds as a basic tenet that the central purpose for schooling is to support every student in reaching her or his highest potential in all areas of growth and development. School practices prepare students to care for themselves and their families, to identify with and make valuable contributions to the local community and the nation in carrying out civic and social responsibilities. A central function of schools is preserving, maintaining, and perpetuating core values of the society, including freedom, equality, justice, and diversity. Schools are responsible for preserving aspects of students' cultural heritage that provide a sense of personal/group identity and place in the world, and that give direction and hope for the future.

Two essential principles are at the core of teaching with purpose. First, the essential purpose for academic knowledge included in the school curriculum is to improve and preserve the quality of life for all people locally, nationally, and globally. Second, subject matter included in the school curriculum is applicable to everyday life in the present and in the future. For example, every subject area and the associated academic skills learned in the classroom are included in an occupation or profession. The focus of the discussion in the remainder of this chapter is on the application of these two principles in the process of developing an approach to teaching with purpose.

Teaching with purpose requires a well-articulated conceptualization of teaching practice. In this discussion, teaching is conceptualized as a scientific-based *interpretive process* that systematically incorporates knowledge about learners, learning, subject matter, and pedagogy to support the growth and development of learners (Hollins, 2011). Basic characteristics of science related to teaching as an interpretive process include but are not limited to: (a) systematic research-based protocols for practice and inquiry; (b) basic principles established through systematic investigation; (c) basic concepts directly related to established principles; and (d) disciplinary discourse with specific language, ways of representing ideas, and ways of thinking.

Teaching as an interpretive process involves fusing *knowledge for practice* that includes a grounded understanding of learning, specific learners, pedagogy, and subject matter in planning learning experiences that are context-specific and characterized by a developmental progression. This interpretive process involves a cycle of applying *knowledge for practice* in planning learning experiences, engaging students in learning, observing and interpreting students' responses when they are engaged in the learning experience, and translating the observed responses for the next iteration of planned learning experiences. This teaching cycle (Figure 2.2) is a macrostructure that reveals the interrelatedness among the elements of teaching practice.

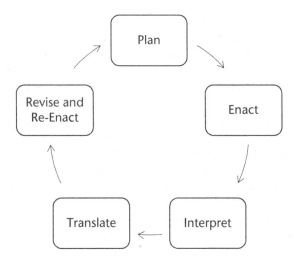

**FIGURE 2.2** Teaching cycle

In teaching as an interpretive process, knowledge of students means understanding the collective knowledge of a group, knowledge held in common
among members of a group, patterns of knowledge within a group, and individual experiences, values, practices, prior school experiences and knowledge,
and knowledge acquired outside of school. Knowledge of students includes
recognizing their talents, strengths, weaknesses, preferences, and gaps in knowledge and skills. Further, it is important to be familiar with the communities
where students live, including the demographic composition, resources, values,
practices, and challenges. Developing grounded knowledge of students requires
a systematic approach such as that described in Chapter 5 in this book.

In teaching as an interpretive process, knowledge of learning refers to both
a theoretical perspective and a learning cycle (Figure 2.3). Discussion of a theoretical perspective on learning will occur later in this chapter. This discussion
will focus on a learning cycle. A learning cycle is a progression of experiences
through which a student develops and internalizes understanding of a concept,
principle, phenomenon, process, or skill. There are different ways to conceptu-
alize a learning cycle; however, the purpose of a learning cycle is to provide a
macrostructure for planning a learning segment or sequence. The macrostructure
of a learning cycle shows the interrelatedness of parts within the segment or
sequence. For example, a learning cycle might include a chain of actions such as
analysis-inquiry-interpretation-application-extrapolation. The actions within this
chain are interrelated and interdependent. Using this chain of actions, a student
observes a phenomenon or reads an account that raises issues for inquiry. The
student conducts the inquiry and applies the finding from the inquiry to practice.
Further, the student interprets and applies the knowledge from the application to

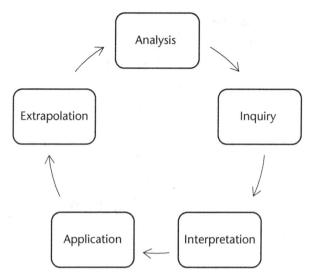

**FIGURE 2.3** Learning cycle

practice in new or novel situations or develops new questions for investigation (extrapolation). Each action in this learning cycle deepens the student's knowledge and provides opportunities for the teacher to check understanding and to monitor progress.

Pedagogical knowledge is an important element of teaching as an interpretive process. Teaching as an interpretive process requires infusing knowledge of pedagogy and subject matter with knowledge of students, embedded within teaching and learning cycles. The teaching and learning cycles are macrostructures for pedagogical practices. The three categories of pedagogical knowledge include declarative, procedural, and conditional. These different categories indicate types and uses of pedagogical knowledge. Declarative knowledge is conceptual or theoretical and has explanatory or predictive properties. Procedural knowledge applies principles, rules, and theories in guiding specific pedagogical actions. Conditional knowledge contextualizes declarative and procedural knowledge in pedagogical practices designed for specific students and specific situations. Procedural knowledge for pedagogical practices can be organized into five categories, including direct instruction, indirect instruction, interactive instruction, experiential learning, and independent learning. The five essential tools for learning that serve as the channel for designing learning experiences are cognition, culture, experience, language, and literacy (Figure 2.4). Employing the appropriate pedagogical procedures, consistent use of the teaching and learning cycles, and contextualized pedagogy increase the probability for access to high-quality learning experiences for urban and underserved students.

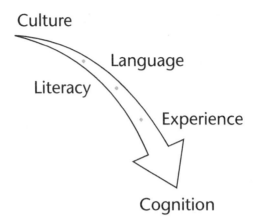

**FIGURE 2.4** Five essential tools

The final element in teaching as an interpretive process is subject matter knowledge. There are specific ways of presenting subject matter to make it accessible and meaningful for students, such as explicating the organizing ideas, concepts, principles, practices, and procedures; language and discourse practices; methods of inquiry and the generation of new knowledge; roles and responsibilities; and application to everyday life, including careers and leisure time activities. Teaching as an interpretive process requires the ability to frame subject matter within the context of what students already know and have experienced, and to extend their knowledge based on their needs, aspirations, and interests.

Your purpose for teaching interprets and applies your philosophical stance. Your purpose for teaching is a way of thinking about the value and impact of teaching on the students in your classroom, the local community, and the larger society. A statement of purpose for teaching is a well-articulated position that addresses how learners will benefit from specific subject matter and learning experiences in the present and in the future, and how academic knowledge applies to everyday life in the local community and the nation. A statement of purpose for teaching is the *contextual framework* for the curriculum, pedagogical practices, application of school policies and procedures, and interactions with students, parents, stakeholders, and the community. It is a commitment to specific actions and intended outcomes.

Teaching with purpose requires specific knowledge of the school and school district where you are employed. This includes knowledge of policies, practices, social context, outcomes, student demographics, and characteristics. This information is available on school and district websites, the website for the state Department of Education, and on the website for the U.S. Department of Education at https://nces.ed.gov/ccd/schoolsearch/school_detail.asp?ID=483237009177.

Data on the academic performance of students and the social context of a school (suspensions, expulsions, referrals to law enforcement, and school-related arrests) are indicators of conditions that influence curriculum framing and pedagogical practices (see Chapter 5).

Teaching with purpose requires knowledge of the local community (Table 2.1) related to its history, demographic composition, assets, and challenges. Every community has assets, opportunities, challenges, and persons and organizations that provide leadership. Examples of assets include people, public facilities and services, historical landmarks, and service organizations. Community assets provide resources for formal and informal learning for children and youth, and serve individual and family needs. Understanding the culture and demographic composition of the local community and school supports contextualizing the curriculum and promoting solidarity among residents. Community-based organizations, governmental agencies, political organizations, and local citizens' community improvement efforts provide opportunities for students to develop values related to civic engagement. Examples of challenges faced by some communities include environmental pollution, public transportation, low income, unemployment, drug addiction, and crime. Some community challenges are appropriate for including in the curriculum as inquiry and community action projects for students. For example, in a science class, students can study environmental pollution and write a letter to the appropriate local governmental agency, or study drug addiction and develop information for distribution in the local community. These assignments contextualize and deepen academic knowledge by providing opportunities for students to apply their knowledge to addressing real-life situations.

## Identifying a Theoretical Perspective

A philosophical stance explains how you understand and think about your work as a teacher, how your work fits into a larger scheme of the social order, your potential impact on students and the social order, and how the society values your work. Your statement of purpose is the *contextual framework* for planning instruction and learning experiences for students. It explains the specific benefit intended for the students you will teach, the community where they live, and the nation. The theoretical perspective you choose, or the one employed at your school, explains how students learn. A theoretical perspective on learning guides the development of learning experiences for students. It supports translating knowledge about students, pedagogy, and subject matter for application in planning and adjusting learning experiences, and making and interpreting observations about students' responses to learning experiences.

Theories of learning constitute one aspect of education science. Education science is an organized and systematized body of knowledge based on verifiable evidence and derived from research incorporating experimentation and observation. Education science identifies observable relationships in patterns of

**TABLE 2.1** Community profile

| | Assets/status | Opportunities | Challenges | Representation (persons and organizations) |
|---|---|---|---|---|
| General description of community | | | | |
| Ethnic/racial composition of community | | | | |
| Historical | | | | |
| Economic (employment, unemployment, sector) | | | | |
| Political (local, state, national) | | | | |
| Social, entertainment | | | | |
| Educational (achievement, attainment, availability) | | | | |
| Health (facilities and resources) | | | | |
| Recreational (facilities and resources) | | | | |
| Environmental | | | | |

factors influencing approaches, conditions, situations, and outcomes of practices. The practice of science in education is important for understanding the conditions under which certain pedagogical practices and school policies are most likely to be effective, evaluating existing practices, interpreting outcomes for specific practices, and improving the effectiveness of practices. In the short term, it may not be possible to validate every pedagogical practice in this way. However, teaching as an interpretive process, as described earlier in this chapter, draws upon the disciplinary practices of science in the teaching cycle, which is an observation-interpretation-translation cycle for improving learning experiences for students. The consistent application of the teaching and learning cycles enables teachers to construct deep knowledge of observable patterns in the classroom related to social relationships, responses to specific learning experiences, gaps in knowledge, and preferences for learning. A theoretical perspective on learning enhances the ability to interpret, translate, and apply knowledge from classroom observations to practice for improving learning outcomes.

There are many theoretical perspectives on learning from which to choose, including behaviorism, cognitivism, and sociocultural theories. These theories are complex and take a great deal of time and effort for developing the depth of understanding necessary for application to practice. Sociocultural theoretical perspectives on learning tend to be more compatible with the philosophical perspective, purpose for teaching, and situating the curriculum as discussed in this chapter. The following description of sociocultural perspectives will provide insight into the application to practice within the context of the discussion in this chapter.

A theoretical perspective is important for understanding the relationship among student characteristics (experiences, knowledge, preferences, and values) and pedagogical practices (situating the curriculum in context, applying epistemic practices, and creating a supportive social context). In the sociocultural perspective represented in this discussion, learning or knowledge construction is cognitive (involving intellectual and mental processes), academic (including the formal school curriculum), and social (cultural, historical, and co-constructed with others). Mental processes develop through socialization into a distinct culture. This socialization process begins at birth and continues throughout life, supported by engaging in social discourse with others in the immediate environment. The social discourse includes learning the language, cultural practices, values, and habits of mind of members of a social or cultural group. In this way, culture mediates cognition through social discourse. Classroom and school practices contribute to the development of higher intellectual or mental functioning. Higher mental functioning involves language, memory, thinking, attention, abstraction, and perception.

Developing the higher intellectual and mental functioning of learners is a process of building upon and extending the cognitive schemata that are already emerging. This is a process of cognitive mediation similar to what occurs through social discourse beginning at birth. The teaching practices that serve to mediate cognition for learning include framing the curriculum and selecting appropriate pedagogical approaches. Positioning academic knowledge and skills within what learners know, their experiences and values increases access and the ability to achieve learning goals.

An example of an approach for applying the sociocultural perspective that incorporates mediated cognition is found in Carol Lee's (1995) use of a culturally based cognitive apprenticeship model for teaching African American high school students how to interpret complex literary text. The students were all familiar with the use of "signifying" in the African American vernacular. Signifying is a complex form of social discourse with metaphorical language that incorporates double entendre, innuendo, irony, and satire in communicating a single message directed to or about an individual or group. A group of African American students in an experimental group were instructed to interpret a passage with dialogue that incorporated signifying. Students were asked to explain the strategy used to infer meaning from the passage. The students developed a set of criteria for making inferences about the deeper meaning of the words used in the passage. The clues and strategies the students used were similar to those used by expert readers to interpret figurative language in complex literary text.

The application of a sociocultural perspective in culturally mediated instruction is clearly evident with Lee's (1995) experimental group. First, the learning experience built upon and extended knowledge developed in the students' everyday cultural experiences. Second, knowledge distributed across the group was used in a *joint productivity activity* to *co-construct* criteria for making inferences from text containing language with double meaning. Third, the students' home culture and language were used to mediate learning approaches for interpreting complex literary text. The skills produced through this culturally mediated approach are applicable when interpreting other text and are comparable to those used by expert readers.

A second example is the use of the language experience approach to teaching early reading skills to third grade children (Dorr, 2006; Hoffman & Roser, 2012). The language experience approach to literacy development engages young children in conversations about a familiar experience or observation with a focus on the relationship between spoken and written language. In the lesson described in Dorr (2006), the teacher brought attention to this relationship through supporting the children in developing clarity in spoken language by describing or labeling objects, situations, or events. The shared experience in this lesson was grocery shopping with parents. While the children were engaged in describing or labeling aspects of their shopping experience, the teacher produced a written form of one word from the discussion. The children associated the word with its referent. The teacher asked the children to repeat a sentence from the discussion of their experience at the grocery store that used the word. The teacher recorded the sentence so that children could make the connection between the spoken and written sentence. The children read the sentence aloud. The children worked in small groups to construct sentences that the whole class used in jointly constructing a paragraph that described an aspect of an experience at a grocery store.

The language experience approach is an example of the use of sociocultural perspective in culturally mediated instruction in the primary grades. The teacher built upon and extended the children's knowledge of a shared cultural experience. Then, knowledge of this experience was used to mediate the literacy development process.

In summary, a theoretical perspective on learning is an important aspect of the science of education that supports interpreting and translating knowledge about students, pedagogy, and subject matter for planning meaningful and productive learning experiences. A theoretical perspective explains the relationship among pedagogical practices, student engagement, and learning outcomes. The example from research conducted by Lee (1995) illustrates the application of a sociocultural perspective in culturally mediated instruction where students use their own culture-specific language as text and context for developing criteria for interpreting complex literary text.

## Situating the Curriculum within Context

The examples of a sociocultural perspective in culturally mediated instruction found in a culturally based cognitive apprenticeship (Lee, 1995) and the language experience approach (Dorr, 2006; Hoffman & Rosen, 2012) are examples of academic skills situated within the context of what students know, what they have experienced, and what they value. Situating academic knowledge within context builds upon and extends culturally mediated instructional strategies for academic skills learned by individual students to include consideration for how students benefit from academic knowledge in the present and the future, and the benefit provided for the local community and the nation. Further, situating academic knowledge within context requires that students learn disciplinary practices, roles, and the ethical standards governing discipline-specific and professional practices.

In this discussion, the teaching of history is consistent with the sociocultural theoretical perspective and the four components of the philosophical stance discussed earlier in this chapter. The philosophical stance addresses the national and community benefit for history teaching and learning, personal connections for students, and practitioner commitments and responsibilities. The sociocultural theoretical perspective guides framing the curriculum and designing learning experiences. Situating the curriculum within context is a process for making the framing and presentation of the curriculum consistent with the philosophical stance and theoretical perspective. Situating the curriculum within the larger context of the purpose of schooling connects with an aspect of your philosophical stance. For example, one aspect of the purpose of schooling embedded within the curriculum is socializing students into national core values, traditions, and ideological, moral, and ethical perspectives. The philosophical stance is the broader perspective in which the purpose for teaching is located that generated the expected outcomes and impact of student learning.

The purpose for teaching is an important element in a philosophical stance. The purpose for teaching history is for students to develop deep understanding of multiple issues that inform active and responsible participation in a democratic society. These issues include understanding: (a) the accomplishments, challenges, and traditions of the past; (b) how the past influences the present and the future; (c) the relationship between national and local history; (d) contemporary social challenges and the role of individual citizens in addressing social challenges; and (e) ways to take personal action and responsibility for addressing contemporary social challenges.

Studying history provides opportunities for students to examine moral and ethical perspectives and appropriate and accepted social norms at different points in time. Examining changes in societal norms over time helps students understand and explain how change happens and options for responding. Studying history supports students in developing a personal and group identity, and in developing for themselves a location within the national identity. Incorporating authentic disciplinary practices in teaching history introduces students to the work of professional practitioners in the field and supports students in identifying possible career options.

Situating curriculum within context reveals the complexity of historical issues and problems. Connecting state and national events with local events and landmarks within the social and political context of the time illuminates the interrelatedness of a chain of events. Examining a chain of events by using multiple sources that incorporate multiple perspectives contributes to a deeper understanding of the events and the impact on different segments of the population, including on the daily lives of individuals living through a specific chain of events. Analyzing changes in laws, policies, and practices linked to a chain of events provides insights into long-term and short-term effects.

An element of situating the curriculum within context is providing students with knowledge about the work done by professionals in a specific discipline. The profile of the class, school, and the local community provided in this chapter indicate that students need academic knowledge and skills, and knowledge of employment opportunities associated with specific disciplines. Information about professions in the discipline will enable students to identify and make connections with individuals in specific roles in the local community (Table 2.2). This information will constitute part of the knowledge base for making career decisions and support aspirations for higher levels of educational attainment. The local community directly benefits economically, politically, and socially when residents have higher levels of educational attainment.

The American Historical Association (www.historians.org) has identified several categories of employment for students of history, including classroom

**TABLE 2.2** Discipline-specific practices

|  | *History* | *Science* |
| --- | --- | --- |
| **Purpose for practice** | Developing historical interpretations, explaining the past | Revealing nature, identifying patterns in nature, explaining nature |
| **Social aspects of practice** | Argumentation | Argumentation |
| **Roles** | Constructor of claims, critiquer | Constructor of claims, critiquer |
| **Practices** | Document analysis, sourcing, contextualization, corroboration, narration | Experimentation, quantification, representation, exposition |

teaching (schools, colleges, and universities), museums, editing and publishing, archives, historical preservation, governmental agencies (federal, state, and local history), and consultants and contractors. Each category of employment requires deep knowledge in specific areas of history and the skills of the discipline, including knowledge of historical methods (approaches to solving problems in knowledge of the past), understanding the historical context and historiographical context (work done by other historians), using the tools of the trade (primary and secondary sources), and developing compelling written historical accounts. Other skills needed by historians relate to specific roles.

## Selecting and Evaluating Epistemic Practices

The epistemic practices discussed in this part of the chapter incorporate the philosophical stance, purpose for teaching, the theoretical perspective, and situating curriculum in context. Establishing these connections is part of developing coherence, consistency, and continuity in student learning. In this discussion, epistemic practices refer to the authentic practices used by scholars and practitioners in a specific discipline. Using the authentic practices for a specific discipline as pedagogy is important for several reasons. First, the practices associated with a specific discipline are authentic. Students learn the work of practitioners in the discipline, including the language, discourse routines, inquiry, organizational structure of the discipline, and how new knowledge is generated. Second, students learn how knowledge from the discipline applies to their daily lives. Third, disciplinary practices require collaboration with others in the co-construction of new knowledge. Fourth, the knowledge and habits of mind learned for a specific discipline apply to situations in everyday life. That is, using disciplinary practices for different subject matter learning broadens students' knowledge of multiple perspectives and approaches.

Epistemic practices for teaching and learning history apply the practices and tools used by professional historians. Historians are primarily concerned with

**FIGURE 2.5** Historical inquiry

addressing unresolved historical issues and questions. The tools used as sources of evidence for resolving historical issues and problems are primary, secondary, and tertiary sources (Figure 2.5). Primary sources include artifacts, diaries, documents, photographs, autobiographies, and other sources of contemporaneous information. Secondary sources are non-contemporary, and include scholarly books and articles created by individuals who did not experience or have personal knowledge of the issue or problem that is the subject of inquiry. Tertiary sources synthesize or summarize information on an issue or topic based on primary and secondary sources.

Historical inquiry is the approach used to identify evidence for addressing a historical problem or question. This approach involves a clearly stated problem, question, thesis, or hypothesis based on present knowledge, a rationale for the hypothesis that includes possible claims, compilation of evidence confirming or disconfirming claims, identifying and refuting counterclaims, and identifying questions for testing the claims. Historians tend to ask complex questions that explain what happened in a situation or event, why an event occurred, the effects of an event or situation, and the role and influence of historical figures, groups, or government agencies. The rationale explains the limitations of knowledge about the problem or question, as well as the importance and implications for understanding the past and the present. Analyzing primary and secondary sources will confirm or disconfirm claims. The historian identifies questions that test the strength of the claims and that suggest areas in need of further investigation. Historians publish their work in books, essays, journal articles, and special reports.

Historiography is an approach to analyzing and synthesizing the work completed on a historical event or historical figure. Historiography is concerned with all aspects of historical scholarship, including the representation of events and historical figures, the methods of inquiry used, and the sources of evidence. Historiographic essays and books are useful resources for identifying problems and questions for inquiry. Historiographic scholarship identifies important historical work, critical debates, consistencies and inconsistencies in accounts and interpretations, and different perspectives. Historiographic traditions take on different perspectives such as feminism, Marxism, social history, intellectual history, cultural history, and others.

Historians use discipline-specific strategies for documenting, representing, and presenting the findings from their work, including argumentation and literacy approaches (Moje, 2007). The written account of historical inquiry results in argumentation or historical narratives. Argumentation is the process through which historians support claims regarding a problem or question by developing a thesis (hypothesis), presenting relevant evidence based on primary and secondary sources, presenting a rationale for each aspect of a claim, and identifying and refuting counterclaims. A historical narrative is a storytelling approach to representing an event, situation, or personality. A historical narrative employs a technique of extrapolation based on evidence from primary and secondary sources, and knowledge of the social and political context of the time. Examples of historical narratives include biographies, autobiographies, and historical fiction.

The tools of the trade for historians are effective as epistemic practices for teaching history in elementary and secondary schools when employed within the context of teaching with purpose. Performance assessments revealing that students have met academic curriculum standards for knowledge, practices, and skills indicate the effectiveness of an epistemic practice. The performance assessment indicates the extent to which students understand the interrelatedness of concepts, the application of principles, how to complete procedures and processes, and how to conduct discipline-specific inquiry. The performance assessment is an indicator of how well students have learned to engage in the discourse and practices of the discipline.

## Understanding the Teaching Process

The teaching process is an overarching conceptualization of the professional practice of teachers. The teaching process explains the rudimentary behaviors and habits of mind that guide professional practice in the field. The discussion in this chapter represents teaching as an interpretive process supported by the core concept of a teaching cycle. The teaching cycle is an iterative process that consists of planning, enacting, interpreting, translating, revising, and re-enacting as necessary. This iterative process is a developmental progression of teaching and learning. Each iteration of the teaching cycle advances the teacher's knowledge of how to support learning for individuals and groups of students and improves the quality of learning experiences for all students.

The first part of the planning phase in the teaching cycle is focused inquiry into students' prior knowledge and experiences and the local community. An earlier discussion in this chapter presented a protocol for developing a community profile. The second part of the planning phase of the teaching cycle is synthesizing and incorporating information about learners and their communities, theories of learning and the learning cycle, curriculum content, and pedagogy to develop contextualized knowledge and meaningful and productive learning experiences.

The second phase in the teaching cycle is enacting contextualized knowledge and meaningful and productive learning experiences. The basis for social arrangements for learning (individual, small group, whole class, etc.) is the confluence of knowledge of students, a theoretical perspective on learning, the learning cycle, epistemic practices, and the expected learning outcomes. The knowledge students develop builds upon and extends what they already know and have experienced, is powerful enough to support subsequent related learning, and is applicable in everyday life in the present and future.

The third phase in the teaching cycle is observing and interpreting students' responses to the enactment of contextualized knowledge and learning experiences. Observing students' responses involves noting levels of engagement, disengagement, questions, understanding, and emotional and social reactions. The basis for interpreting students' responses is your understanding of students, their prior knowledge and experiences, the theoretical perspective, subject matter knowledge, epistemic practices, and social arrangements. Interpreting students' responses is a process of locating and identifying confusion or misunderstanding, and negative emotional and social responses. Examples of challenges for students include misunderstandings and gaps in prior knowledge, weak connections between subject matter and prior knowledge and experiences, uncomfortableness with subject matter, inadequate knowledge for completing part of the learning cycle, inappropriate sequencing of knowledge or learning experiences, and inappropriate social arrangements.

The fourth phase in the teaching cycle is translating students' responses for revising and re-enacting learning experiences, if necessary. Translating students' responses is a process for determining appropriate adjustments in teaching practices and learning experiences. The location and identification of challenges form the basis for adjustments. Examples of adjustments include teaching prerequisite knowledge and skills, making stronger connections between subject matter and prior knowledge and experiences, reframing aspects of subject matter or learning experiences to increase comfortableness, teaching the skills necessary for completing the learning cycle, altering the sequence of knowledge or learning experiences, and changing the social arrangements.

The fifth phase of the teaching cycle incorporates adjustments for practice into revisions for re-enacting a learning cycle, or applying knowledge gained from the previous teaching cycle in presenting a new learning cycle. This fifth phase of the teaching cycle is the beginning of a new teaching cycle, and a subsequent iteration of the teaching process. Each phase in this iterative teaching process contributes to the continuous effectiveness and quality of learning experiences for all students. Methodically observing, analyzing, and adjusting learning experiences based on each student's responses ensures equity and quality for all students.

## Application to Practice

The basic responsibility for the teaching profession is to ensure that every student reaches her or his highest potential and develops the competence and skills necessary to provide for self and family, and to actively participate in and contribute to the well-being of the local community and the nation. A persistent challenge for teachers is providing equitable access to high-quality, meaningful, and productive learning experiences for traditionally underserved students. The discussion in this chapter presented a conceptual model for *teaching with purpose*. This conceptual model supports thinking about and planning meaningful and productive learning experiences and a comfortable and supportive social context for learning. The conceptual model has five frames of practices that include a philosophical stance, a theoretical perspective, curriculum situated in context, epistemic practices, and a teaching process.

Application of the conceptual model for *teaching with purpose* requires an intentionally planned interconnectedness among the philosophical stance, theoretical perspective, and the teaching process. This intentional interconnectedness among the philosophical stance, theoretical perspective, and the teaching process forms the basis for the curriculum and pedagogical practices (epistemic practices). The curriculum and epistemic practices provide evidence for application of the foundational philosophy, theory, and process (Table 2.3).

Developing meaningful and productive learning experiences depends on deep knowledge of students and the local community. Chapter 3 addresses the knowledge of students needed for meaningful and productive teaching and learning.

**TABLE 2.3** Application of model for teaching with purpose

|  | Curriculum | Epistemic practices |
| --- | --- | --- |
| Philosophical stance |  |  |
| Theoretical perspective |  |  |
| Teaching process |  |  |

**TABLE 2.4** Application of community profile

| Community | Curriculum | Learning experiences |
|---|---|---|
| Assets | | |
| Challenges | | |
| Values | | |

The discussion in this chapter included a protocol for developing a community profile. Incorporating information from the community profile related to assets, challenges, and values into the curriculum and learning experiences provides evidence for implementing the model for *teaching with purpose* (Table 2.4).

The discussion in this chapter presented teaching as an interpretive process that requires systematically implementing a teaching cycle. Consistently employing all five phases of the teaching cycle ensures that every student has an equitable opportunity for meaningful and productive learning experiences.

## Chapter Summary

The conceptual model for *teaching with purpose* presented in this chapter is a response to the data on disparities in learning outcomes, educational attainment, and household income based on ethnicity, race, and social class status presented in Chapter 1. The conceptual model for *teaching with purpose* aims to increase the coherence, continuity, and quality of learning experiences provided for all students, especially urban and underserved students. High-quality learning experiences prepare students with the competency and skills necessary for providing for themselves and their families, and for contributing to their communities and the nation.

This chapter presented an approach to *teaching with purpose* based on a conceptual model consisting of a philosophical stance, theoretical perspective, contextualized school curriculum, epistemic practices, and a teaching process. The interconnectedness among the philosophical stance, theoretical perspective, and the teaching process is foundational for the curriculum and pedagogical practices (epistemic practices). The curriculum and epistemic practices provide evidence that the philosophical stance, theoretical perspective, and teaching process are applied. Deep knowledge of students and the local community support contextualizing the curriculum and epistemic practices.

The discussion in this chapter represented professional teaching practice as an interpretive process supported by teaching and learning cycles. The teaching cycle is an iterative process that consists of five phases that include planning, enacting, interpreting, translating, revising, and re-enacting as necessary. The teaching cycle illuminates the importance of meticulous planning, focused observation, documentation of students' responses to learning experiences, and adjustments in learning experiences based on students' responses. The learning cycle involves analysis, inquiry, interpretation, application, and extrapolation. The learning cycle fosters science-based habits of mind and deep knowledge of subject matter for students. Further, the learning cycle provides opportunities for observing students' responses to subject matter and learning experiences.

## References

Dewey, J. (1897). My pedagogic creed. *School Journal*, 54, 77–80. Retrieved from http://dewey.pragmatism.org/creed.htm.

Dorr, R. E. (2006). Something old is new again: Revisiting language experience. *The Reading Teacher*, 60(2), 138–146.

Hoffman, J. V. & Roser, N. (2012). Reading and writing the world using beautiful books: Language experience re-envisioned. *Language Arts*, 89(5), 293–304.

Hollins, E. R. (2011). Teacher preparation for quality teaching. *Journal of Teacher Education*, 62(4), 395–407.

Lee, C. D. (1995). A culturally based cognitive apprenticeship: Teaching African American high school students skills in literary interpretation. *Reading Research Quarterly*, 30(4), 608–630.

National Association for the Education of Young Children (NAEYC) Code of Ethical Conduct and Statement of Commitment. Retrieved from www.naeyc.org/files/naeyc/image/public_policy/Ethics%20Position%20Statement2011_09202013update.pdf.

National Association of State Directors of Teacher Education and Certification (NASDTEC) model code of ethics for educators. Retrieved from www.nasdtec.net/?page=MCEE_Doc.

# 3

# TEACHING FROM THE CENTER

## Focus Questions

1. How does *teaching from the center* differ from existing approaches to classroom teaching and learning in perspective and practice?
2. What are the most salient factors in *teaching from the center*?
3. How is the academic performance of adolescents and children of color influenced by racism and racial identity?

## Introduction

*Teaching from the center* means using essential knowledge about students, their everyday experiences and observations in the home and community, and their cultural and ancestral knowledge in framing the curriculum and designing learning experiences. *Teaching from the center* requires knowledge of the context in which the child's character and cognition develop—the influence of the context on the formation of the person. Teaching from the center requires academic and professional knowledge of child and adolescent growth and development to inform practices that support learners in reaching their highest potential. The pedagogy in teaching from the center is located within, builds upon, and deepens knowledge of cultural practices and values. Students build upon and extend their home language to advance the effectiveness of oral and written communication. The local community is the context and text for academic learning (Figure 3.1).

The model for *teaching with purpose* described in Chapter 2 is requisite for using the essential knowledge for *teaching from the center*. The use of essential knowledge about students informs and is informed by the philosophical stance,

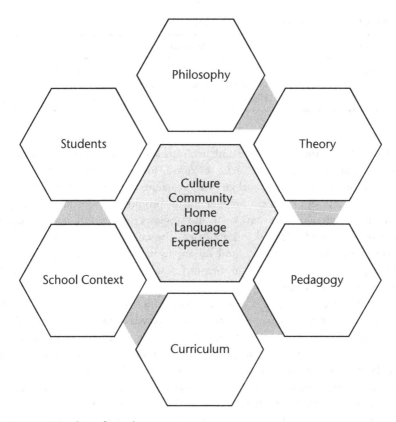

**FIGURE 3.1** Teaching from the center

theoretical perspective, and situating the curriculum within the community context. The philosophical stance or purpose for teaching, presented in the previous chapter, supports students in constructing deep and powerful knowledge that is useful in everyday life, preparing for the future, and for improving life in the local community. The theoretical perspective on learning takes into consideration the fact that ways of knowing and ways of learning originate in ancestral knowledge passed from one generation to the next across many generations. At the core, learning differences link to culture and socialization practices.

This chapter presents four themes. First, understanding child and adolescent development for children of color living in a racialized society. Second, framing the curriculum in ways that connect students with their cultural heritage, including ways of knowing and ways of learning. Third, understanding the community as context and text for learning. This includes learning about the community and learning specific subject matter within the context of community resources. Fourth, using students' culture, heritage, and experiences in pedagogy.

**TABLE 3.1** Culture: an essential tool for learning

| Making meaning | Interpreting the world |
| --- | --- |
| Representation | Symbolic representation of meaning (language) |
| Practices | Ways of interacting with the world |
| Values | Beliefs and priorities based on understanding of the world |

In teaching from the center, students learn about the meaning of culture in framing human behavior and social discourse, their own cultures, the cultures of peers, and the shared national culture. Teaching from the center supports the cultural identity development for individuals, promotes acceptance and respect for cultures different from one's own, and supports the development of a shared national cultural identity. In this approach, the cultural values inherent in the school curriculum are explicit. Students are aware of the purpose, perspectives, philosophical stance, and the prioritizing of ways of knowing present in the school curriculum (Table 3.1).

Teaching from the center contextualizes learning within the culture, cultural heritage, cognition, language, literacy, and everyday experiences of students. The curriculum includes the history, traditions, and accomplishments of the ancestors, previous and current generations of students. Students learn to identify claims, counterclaims, different perspectives, and different ways of knowing. Students learn to make connections among knowledge in the school curriculum, their personal experiences, plans for the future, cultural perspectives, and ancestral knowledge. This interconnectedness of knowledge across the spectrum of ways of life past, present, and future provides a basis for understanding and living with human differences and advancing the quality of existence for all life on the planet.

## Contextualizing Child and Adolescent Growth and Development

Teaching from the center requires a deep understanding of child and adolescent growth and development as it relates to ethnic minority children of color in the United States. There are particular factors that threaten the healthy mental and physical development of children of color, including those who are immigrants, that appear less threatening to the development of mainstream middle-class children. These factors involve social class, ethnicity, culture, and race located within a system of social stratification based on racism, prejudice, discrimination, oppression, and segregation. Garcia Coll et al. (1996) presented an integrative model for the study of developmental competencies in minority children comprised of eight factors that influence the potential for healthy growth and development for children of color, including social position, racism, segregation, promoting/inhibiting environments, adaptive culture, child characteristics, family, and developmental competencies. These factors frame and limit the opportunities provided for minority children and youth, and produce stress and tension that threaten the healthy growth and development of children of color living within and outside the urban core.

The following discussion describes the intersection of societal factors, child development, school practices, and teaching and learning for children of color. This discussion is organized around three phases in the children's development, early childhood (PK–grade 3), preadolescence (grades 4–8), and adolescence (grades 9–12). This discussion addresses the role of the teacher as patron and advocate in guiding and monitoring the child's progress in each phase.

## Early Childhood (PK–Grade 3)

Children of color enter school while engaged in an enculturation process at home. Children are learning who they are and how they fit into the world. During the enculturation process, children learn the language spoken by their parents or caregivers, and engage in a cognitive apprenticeship where they learn how to think about and make sense of the world, including how to identify and label phenomena in the environment. Further, children learn the values and perceptions of those in their home environment and the larger society. Through the media and social contact within and outside the family, many children learn the value of race, skin color, and social status by the time they are 4 or 5 years old, and darker-skinned children are feeling the impact (Lewis, 2003; Van Ausdale & Feagin, 2001). This socialization process contributes to developing self-esteem and self-confidence, factors that support the development of academic and intellectual competence.

Based on traditional school practices, children of color learn that they are valued less than their peers who are White, and lighter-skinned children experience more favorable treatment than their peers who have darker skin. This is observable in classrooms and on playgrounds in preschools and elementary schools (Lewis, 2003; Van Ausdale & Feagin, 2001). Many children of color come to view themselves as less academically capable and less deserving of benefits and privileges in comparison to their White peers. School policies and practices reinforce feelings of low self-confidence and low self-esteem in children of color. The traditional school curriculum only occasionally acknowledges the presence of people of color in society. However, public reports on the academic performance and school discipline for elementary and high school students disaggregate outcomes by race and ethnicity (NAEP, 2014). For example, data from the U.S. Department of Education, Office of Civil Rights (2014) show that in 2011–2012, African American children in preschool disproportionately received out-of-school suspensions as compared to their White peers. African American children comprise 18% of preschool enrollment, but they receive 42% of single out-of-school suspensions and 48% of multiple out-of-school suspensions. In contrast,

White children comprise 43% of preschool enrollment, and receive 28% of single out-of-school suspensions and 26% of multiple out-of-school suspensions.

It is important to point out that the experiences children of color have in early childhood frame how they understand school and their place in it. For many children of color, school is a very hostile, stressful, and lonely experience faced without adequate guidance and support from adults within or outside of school. Children respond to this circumstance in different ways. Some children withdraw and are silent in an attempt to avoid additional punishment or uncomfortableness, while others act out in an attempt to bring attention to their pain (Garcia Coll et al., 1996). These approaches are unlikely to bring relief. Often adults ignore the withdrawn and silent child. Adults punish the child who acts out and may deprive the child of regular education by placing her or him in special education for a behavior disorder. Behaviorist perspectives guide traditional approaches to school discipline. The approach used by many schools emphasizes constraints and boundaries with related consequences. There is often less attention to guidance and support, or building relationships prior to or after infractions are committed.

A few public, private, and independent schools employ a constructivist or sociocultural perspective, emphasizing inquiry or project-based learning, incorporating knowledge valued in the children's local communities, providing learning experiences that are meaningful for children, focusing on self-regulation and supportive social relationships among all participants. In these schools, teachers and administrators support children in developing a positive cultural and racial identity, appreciation for other cultures, and the social skills that support developing positive relationships with peers and teachers. Teachers act as patrons, advocates, and mentors for children's academic, social, and psychological development, giving particular attention to the needs of children of color and other traditionally underserved students.

## Early and Preadolescence (Grades 4–8)

According to Wentzel (1991), "during early adolescence, students' identification with and conformity to peers increases dramatically" (p. 1067). Peer relationships influence adjustment and performance at school. The quality of peer relationships has a strong influence on emotional and motivational responses to school. Social competence influences the quality of peer relationships among children and in early adolescence. Aspects of social competence include social responsibility, peer relationships, and self-regulatory processes. Low levels of social competence complicates life during early adolescence for children within their own age cohort and ethnic/social groups. Children with low levels of social competence attending schools with peers from diverse cultural and experiential groups are at even higher risks for isolation and exclusion based on bias and prejudice. School-imposed disruptions of peer cohorts by such practices as grade level retention further complicate the social life for children who are different from their peers in race and social class.

Many children have experienced school-imposed disruptions in their peer relationships due to grade level retention and falling behind grade level in reading and math resulting from inflexible pedagogical approaches. The process of grade level retention removes children from their peer cohort and places them in a cohort with children who are one or more years younger, and who have formed bonded peer relationships. Children placed with a younger cohort are subject to teasing and ridicule by children from both the new and the former cohorts. The older children in the cohort may experience isolation and rejection, and feel embarrassed or intimidated to participate or perform in the presence of their peers. Children who have fallen behind in academic skills may have the same experiences as those who have received grade level retention. Isolation, rejection, and feelings of embarrassment can cause significant stress for children. Cohort displacement combined with other differences such as academic ability, physical appearance, physical ability, and racial identity significantly increase children's negative social experiences and stress. Continuous exposure to stress has a negative effect on learning in the classroom, further decreasing the potential benefit from grade level retention and decreasing the possibility for children to catch up who have fallen behind in academic skills.

Children of color experience the additional burden of racial bias, prejudice, and discrimination. Prejudice and discrimination based on race begins in early childhood and continues through adulthood (Lewis, 2003; Van Ausdale & Feagin, 2001; Yip, Sellers, & Seaton, 2006). At the time of preadolescence, many children have developed particular ways of making sense of the world around them and have developed expectations for how school works, especially relationships among peers. Lewis (2001) pointed out that:

> Not only are many lessons learned and taught in the actual curriculum, but schools (and school personnel) also serve as a source of racial information, a location (and means) for interracial interaction, and/or a means of both affirmation of and challenge to previous racial attitudes and understandings.
>
> *(p. 783)*

Lewis (2001) indicates that the school curriculum reinforces race-based power relationships through the omission and biased representation of people of color, especially in teaching the history of the United States. The disproportionate administration of harsh discipline to children of color as compared to their White peers, as well as disparities in learning outcomes, further reinforce bias and prejudiced perceptions. In school situations that involve children from diverse cultural and experiential backgrounds, children of color often experience name-calling, isolation, and exclusion based on race. In schools that are monoracial with children of color, skin color becomes the basis for prejudice and discrimination. This is an example of internalized racism learned through the school curriculum and social media. According to Lewis (2001), "school personnel's limited interventions or downplaying of such incidents do little to address the anxiety and upset of those who are victims of this hurtful behavior" (p. 790).

Competent and sensitive adult intervention can ameliorate negative peer relationships and academic challenges children encounter. Children in early and preadolescence spend more time with classroom teachers than with their parents. Consequently, teachers have more opportunities to observe children's academic, social, and psychological development and to provide guidance than do their parents. Teachers have an obligation to intervene and support children observed struggling with social skills, or with isolation and rejection by their peers.

## Adolescence (Grades 9–12)

A central task in adolescence is identity formation (Harper, 2007). The task of identity formation involves the process of locating oneself in the world past, present, and future. The challenge for many adolescents is developing an integrated and positive identity that will endure over time and place, conditions and situations, and that supports positive self-esteem and good mental health. Additionally, adolescents of color need an ethnic or racial identity that mitigates the harmful effects of prejudice, racism, and discrimination.

Children and adolescents receive a multitude of social messages about race, racial status, and racial preferences from interacting with their peers and people from their own racial groups, members of other racial groups, and the media. When internalized, these messages become part of the way children and adolescents understand their place in the world in relationship to other people. Developing a positive racial identity in the midst of negative messages about their race is a significant challenge for adolescents of color. DeCuir-Gunby (2009) described Black racial identity as "the attitudes and beliefs that an African American has about his or her belonging to the Black race individually, the Black race collectively, and their perception of other racial groups" (p. 103). The messages students receive from the school curriculum, pedagogical practices, school discipline practices, and learning outcomes do not support positive racial identity development for many urban children and adolescents. Harper (2007) pointed out that the deficit perspective guiding *many* school practices:

> emphasizes an overly controlling, punitive approach to teaching Black students, which undermines the implementation of cooperative and innovative pedagogical practices. It is feasible that these practices, far from encouraging a positive link between Black racial identity and academic achievement, are at least partially responsible for a disruption in the link between urban students' construction of a Black racial identity and academic achievement.
>
> *(p. 232)*

Adolescents from oppressed racial and ethnic groups are at risk for developing a culture of low academic performance in schools that employ a deficit perspective.

## Framing Curriculum for Urban Students

Framing the curriculum to support a positive ethnic and racial identity is essential for urban and other underserved youth. A part of developing personal identity is locating one's self in the curriculum through the accomplishments and traditions of past generations. Students need to understand knowledge as a cultural product and their own ancestors as knowledge producers. More often than not, discipline-specific knowledge in all areas of the curriculum has a historical origin connected to particular individuals and cultural groups. This is apparent in the identification of people from diverse groups who have contributed to discipline-specific knowledge in recent times, as well as the epistemological origins of knowledge and skills in the curriculum. For example, documentation and notation in science are evident where early cultures used pictographs, cuneiform, and hieroglyphics to record events and cultural practices. Incorporating the cultural and epistemological origins of contemporary knowledge into the curriculum facilitates identity development and deepens understanding.

Artifacts, tools, and traditions are symbolic representations of the collective knowledge and wisdom of particular cultural groups. Ancestral knowledge transmitted through oral traditions, song, and formal documentation is an important aspect in the developmental progression of a culture. Examining symbolic representations provides opportunities for students to understand how ideas evolve over time (Li, 2000). DiMaggio and Markus (2010) pointed out that sociologists "increasingly have come to understand culture as comprising social representations, mental models, and ordering schemata . . . and the environmental conditions (institutional arrangements, material culture, media programming) that sustain or challenge them" (p. 349). Cultural groups develop unique ways of communicating and transmitting knowledge from one generation to the next. Language is a cultural product and artifact that serves as a culturally based tool for communication among people who share a common understanding of its meaning and symbols. Several different cultural groups can share the same language, or dialects of the same language, but have difficulty communicating because of variations in cultural perceptions and traditions that influence meaning and the use of symbols. Language supports the transmission of cultural knowledge and wisdom. Tomasello (1999) explained:

> Ontogenetically, human children grow up in the midst of these socially and historically constituted artifacts and traditions, which enables them to (a) benefit from the accumulated knowledge and skills of their social groups; (b) acquire and use perspectivally based cognitive representations in the form of linguistic symbols (and analogies and metaphors constructed from these symbols); and (c) internalize certain types of discourse interactions into skills of metacognition, representational redescription, and dialogic thinking.
>
> (p. 10)

Ancestral knowledge is the cumulative understanding of the world constructed by a particular cultural group from multiple sources over many centuries. Examples of sources for ancestral knowledge include: (a) traditional knowledge passed from generation to generation through oral traditions and documentation in graphic or symbolic forms; (b) empirical knowledge gained from careful and systematic observations of natural phenomena over time; and (c) revealed knowledge acquired through spiritual origins based on cultural beliefs and practices (McGregor, 2004). McGregor (2004) pointed out that "Indigenous knowledge represents an integration of person, place, product, and process" (p. 391). While much of traditional ancestral knowledge focused on subsistence, it had broad applications to law, government, social relationships, health and medicine, philosophy, education, and the environment (Mabit, 2002). Ancestral knowledge transmitted across multiple generations over many centuries embodies the developmental progression and collective knowledge of a particular cultural group.

In studying the cultural historical origins and development of knowledge, it is important for students to understand that catastrophic events in the history of a cultural group can result in ruptures and disruptions in ancestral knowledge. Colonization, enslavement, and war are examples of such catastrophic events. During periods of colonization, enslavement, and war, one group oppresses and discriminates against the other, often demanding the abandonment of ancestral knowledge, language, cultural traditions, and practices. This has been especially true during European expansion (Purcell, 1998). Historically, European colonizers dismissed the ancestral knowledge of indigenous people, referred to as *indigenous knowledge*, as non-scientific (Sillitoe, 1998). Misunderstanding the disruptive impact of catastrophic events on cultural continuity and progress can lead to misperceptions, bias, stereotypes, and prejudice against particular cultural and ethnic groups.

## Providing Equitable Access to Classroom Learning

Beyond framing identity development, cultural values and practices are the context for developing cognitive processes. Cultural traditions, collective knowledge and wisdom, and types of discourse shape thinking, perception, and learning preferences. Varnum, Grossman, Kitayama, and Nisbett (2010) described differences in patterns of thinking and perception in different societies. In some societies, the cognitive orientation is analytical, while in other societies the cognitive orientation is holistic. In differentiating analytic cognition and holistic cognition, the authors pointed out:

> Analytic cognition is characterized by taxonomic and rule-based categorization of objects, a narrow focus in visual attention, dispositional bias in causal attribution, and the use of formal logic in reasoning. In contrast,

holistic cognition is characterized by thematic and family-resemblance-based categorization of objects, a focus on contextual information and relationships in visual attention, an emphasis on situational causes in attribution, and dialecticism.

*(Varnum et al., 2010, p. 9)*

These different patterns of thinking and perception are evident in the everyday discourse of members of particular cultural and ethnic groups. Traditional pedagogical practices are consistent with analytical cognitive processes. Students with a holistic cognitive orientation perform less well with traditional pedagogical approaches than do their peers with an analytical cognitive orientation. Adjustments in pedagogical practices and learning experiences to accommodate a holistic cognitive orientation would benefit many presently underserved students.

Further, ancestral knowledge and shared experiences within a particular social and environmental context constitute collective cultural memory that influences cognitive processes. Collective cultural memory generates:

cognitive processes that produce schemata that define the past. Schemata are "knowledge structures that represent objects or events and provide default assumptions about their characteristics, relationships, and entailments under conditions of incomplete information" (DiMaggio 1997: 269). They are culturally formed and rooted, and constrain and enable thought.

*(Beim, 2007, p. 7)*

Building upon cultural memory, schemata, and cognitive processes deepens understanding and enhances learning.

The power of pedagogy is in making deep connections among ancestral knowledge, the framing of cognition resulting from ancestral knowledge, present contextualized experiential knowledge, and the learning experiences supporting cognitive processing. Western analytic and non-Western holistic cognitive orientations are significant in teaching and learning because each influences a different approach for attending to and processing information. In non-Western holistic thought processes, the understanding of any phenomenon is in relationship to the context in which it is located. Understanding the action or reaction of an individual requires knowledge of the context and social dynamic. In Western analytic thought processes, the understanding of any particular phenomenon is in relationship to its attributes apart from the context. Understanding the action or reaction of an individual requires knowledge of the attributes of the individual, rather than the relationship of the individual to the social context (Beim, 2007). Each cognitive orientation has strengths and weaknesses. This suggests that teaching learners to reach their highest potential requires developing awareness of and competence in both cognitive orientations. The strength of the relationship among the curriculum, pedagogy, support for identity formation, and students' cognitive orientation influences learning outcomes.

Ancestral knowledge informs teaching practices and learning experiences in multiple ways, including: (a) the purpose for learning; (b) cognitive orientation for learning; and (c) designing of learning experiences. Ancestral knowledge is foundational in the formation of students' cognitive processes. Incorporating the cognitive processes inherent in ancestral knowledge into teaching practices boosts and accelerates learning for traditionally underserved students.

The earliest non-Western ancestral knowledge was highly contextualized and role-specific to provide deep knowledge of the local environment to enable human survival. This knowledge passed from one generation to the next, with each iteration increasing in sophistication (Castellano, 2000). The passing of ancestral knowledge from one generation to the next provided for the accumulation of knowledge that supported improvement in the quality of life for subsequent generations. The discussion in Chapter 3 addressed the philosophy and purpose for teaching, which includes improving the quality of life for traditionally underserved students. Students need to understand the application of academic knowledge in everyday life, its value for the future, and its relationship to their ancestral knowledge.

Learning experiences that incorporate ancestral ways of knowing and constructing knowledge, such as careful observation over time, apprenticeship/demonstration, and narrative representations in the form of storytelling and metaphors, support learning for students with a holistic cognitive orientation. Employing Western analytic and non-Western holistic cognitive perspectives in learning experiences increases access for students from diverse cultural and experiential backgrounds. Pedagogical practices can reflect both the Western analytic and the non-Western holistic traditions. For example, a common practice in kindergarten is the morning message, which includes the date and the assignment for the day. The morning message teaches children the days of the week, months of the year, and holistic time markers when children review what happened yesterday, and what will happen today and tomorrow. Introducing holistic time markers in this way helps children learn the documentation function of the calendar while learning the function of print in communicating important information. This is a direct instruction pedagogical approach, which is a product of Western logic applied in teaching. Students of all ages can learn from the apprenticeship approach used in passing ancestral knowledge from one generation to the next. For example, young children can learn to write stories as apprentices for authors of children's books. Middle and high school students can learn to write historical accounts from interacting with historians and to write news articles through interactions with journalists.

The inquiry approach to learning reflects the way ancestral knowledge developed through careful observation over time. Initial forms of notation included the oral tradition of storytelling, songs, and poems. Early forms of symbolic documentation included pictographs, cuneiform, and hieroglyphics. Students can apply the inquiry approach in direct observation of natural phenomena in the study of earth science and indirectly in studying primary documents to construct a historical narrative. When students learn the ancestral sources for the pedagogical approaches that frame their learning experiences, intergenerational connections form that support identity development and cross-cultural appreciation and respect.

## Utilizing the Community as Context and Text for Learning

In local communities, people engage in their everyday lives, and through their actions and interactions they continue many of the traditions of their ancestors in their practices, thought processes, and values. Most communities include different cultural and ethnic groups with different ancestral traditions. Children from these different groups attend school together and eventually share a common language. Over time, members of different cultural and ethnic groups living together in the same community develop a shared history, a collective memory, and share local resources. Members of the community develop shared experiences and interests, especially living conditions and resources. The community context combined with ancestral knowledge in the curriculum and pedagogy further advance the complexity and depth of learning in school. The richness of the diversity and resources in the community contribute to the value of the community as context and text for learning, and as a resource for individual and family life (Schuttenberg & Guth, 2015).

The community is a rich context for academic learning because it is where children grow and develop, and share experiences with family and friends. The community provides richness for learning, cognitive schemata for constructing knowledge, and the setting for the application of academic knowledge. Urban communities are complex places that provide content, object, and substance for inquiry and study. Urban communities are diverse culturally, economically, politically, and socially. However, in many urban communities, the residents disproportionately experience poverty, unemployment, homelessness, poor healthcare, and food insecurity. In many situations, schools are a primary resource for information on community services and resources available for local residents.

Teaching from the center is an approach to transforming schools and communities. This approach requires knowing the local community as a reference point for framing the curriculum and developing meaningful learning experiences that promote academic excellence, active community engagement, and providing guidance and referrals for students to appropriate community resources that address specific needs. The community profile for teaching from the center has four categories, including history and culture, governance, economy, and family, social, and community resources.

### *History and Culture*

Understanding the history and culture of a community is essential for developing deep knowledge of students' cultural traditions, values, and practices. It is important to identify and read a well-documented account of local history. If a well-documented historical account is not available, this is an excellent project for middle and high school students. Otherwise, teachers can collaborate in developing a historical account for use by colleagues and students at the school.

The history and culture are complex for most communities from early settlement to the present—whether the community is monocultural or multicultural, or the population is stable or has undergone patterns of demographic changes over time. The history of the community includes identification of early settlers, the conditions and purpose for the settlement, major events and challenges over time, and the identification of people who participated in and contributed to the development, governance, and maintenance of the community. Community-based organizations are part of the history, governance, and political agency of a community. The Urban League, the National Association for the Advancement of Colored People (NAACP), the Japanese American League (JACL), and the Mexican American Legal Defense Fund (MALDF) are examples of organizations that have a long and rich history of participation in the struggle for social justice. Primary sources of evidence for the history and culture of a people include artifacts in museums, private collections, architecture and other historical markers, and records kept in local libraries, the Library of Congress, and in city repositories.

## Governance

The governance for the community includes the city council, local community councils, city and community boards, and state and federal legislators. Local boards of education are part of the community governance structure. This structure of governance contributes to maintaining the highest possible quality of life through identifying and addressing community needs. The work of boards of education and public school educators impacts every aspect of life in the local community. These governing bodies hold regularly scheduled meetings that are open to the public where residents can make comments and present issues. The agenda and work of these governing bodies represent the priorities and values of the communities they serve to the extent possible given the resources available. Documentation of the agenda and work of these governing bodies is in the minutes of meetings, local newspapers, public records, and in periodic publications available to the public.

Community residents elect most members of the official governing bodies, although elected officials make some appointments. At the state and federal levels, governing bodies are usually partisan. This means that they subscribe to the ideology of a political party—Democrat, Republican, independent, etc. The ideology is usually conservative, independent, or liberal. This ideological perspective has a historical origin. More importantly, this political orientation guides decisions concerning every aspect of community life. It is part of the culture of the community.

Community-based organizations are often a source of social and political influence on the work of official governing bodies. These organizations are nonpartisan but represent particular interests or the interests of particular groups. For example, there are multiple groups addressing issues of social justice, a national interest based on the U.S. Constitution. However, these community-based national organizations usually represent specific groups. One such group is the National Association for the Advancement of Colored People (NAACP). This group has addressed issues of discrimination and segregation at the local, state, and national levels directly related to African American and other populations. These organizations have a long history and many accomplishments, including the NAACP-led fight against race-based school segregation that resulted in the landmark *Brown v. Topeka* Supreme Court decision that such discrimination is unconstitutional. This activism by the NAACP benefitted other ethnic minority and underserved groups subjected to similar discrimination. Similar groups addressing issues of social justice include the Urban League, the Japanese American Citizens League (JACL), and the Mexican American Legal Defense Fund (MALDF). Many of the issues addressed by these groups are related to public education, such as the cases brought by MALDF concerning the education of immigrant and undocumented school-aged children and racial disparities in funding public schools.

The agenda set by governing boards and politically active community-based organizations represents the interests and values of the communities served. Schools operate within this governance structure and are accountable to an elected or appointed governing board that represents the local community. Professional educators are obligated to act in the best interest of the students and community they serve. This includes facilitating students' academic and social development, as well as preparation for active and responsible participation as citizens in the local community. This requires that educators develop deep knowledge of the governance structure, the agenda of governing bodies, and the interests, needs, and values of the local community. This knowledge is essential for guiding the academic and social development of students.

## Economy

The local economy is complex and multidimensional. There are multiple influences on the condition of the economy, including external and local factors. External factors are global, national, and statewide, including employment, wages, inflation, interest rates, and consumer confidence. Local factors influencing the economy include employment, median income, average wages, residential property ownership, educational attainment, and training.

Perhaps the greatest influence on the local economy is the quality of schooling available and the level of educational attainment for the residents. The quality of education available in elementary and secondary schools determines the extent to which students are prepared for higher education or training for the workforce. Low-performing schools do not produce a skilled workforce that attracts and supports major industries that require highly skilled workers for high-paying jobs. Due to inadequate education and the high school dropout rate in urban communities, many local workers are not qualified for high-paying jobs. In 2013, the national high school graduation rate reached 81%; however, many urban high schools graduated less than 60% of entering freshmen. Data from the U.S. Department of Labor, Bureau of Labor Statistics (2017) show that in 2016, those with less than a high school diploma had an unemployment rate of 7.4%, with median weekly earnings of $504. Workers with a high school diploma had an unemployment rate of 5.2% and mean weekly earnings of $692. The unemployment rate is significantly lower for workers with a bachelor's degree (2.7%) and weekly earnings are much higher ($1,156) (Figure 3.2).

Classroom teachers contribute to the level of poverty or wealth in the local community through the quality of instruction provided for the academic and social development of students. Children often enter school with limited exposure to some of the factors that influence academic and cognitive development. Traditional approaches to pedagogy and subject matter may be insufficient for overcoming such factors. However, high-performing, high-minority, high-poverty schools documented by the Education Trust demonstrate that high-quality learning experiences can overcome many negative early childhood experiences in supporting children for performing at or above grade level in reading and mathematics (https://edtrust.org/dispelling_the_myth/). Further, the New Teacher Project (2012) reported that the top-performing teachers in the urban schools included in their study increased learning for students by five to six months beyond that of their lower-performing colleagues. These data

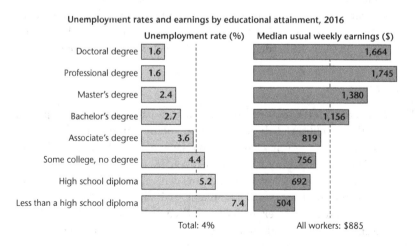

Unemployment rates and earnings by educational attainment, 2016

FIGURE 3.2 Unemployment

show that the commitment and skills of classroom teachers determine students' learning outcomes. Individual and family income depends on the quality and level of educational attainment. The quality of local schools determines the future level of poverty or wealth in a community.

Knowledge of the local economy integrated across the curriculum in most subject areas increases the meaningfulness of classroom learning. Studying the local economy supports students in applying mathematics skills and making connections between academic knowledge and real-world experiences. Studying the local industry and employment patterns supports students in identifying options for future employment. Studying historical patterns in economic market sectors such as the cost of housing helps students apply knowledge of history in interpreting the past and present. Learning experiences related to the local economy are appropriate for all grade levels.

## Health and Human Service in the Community

Community services that support families and other local residents include education, food services, health and recreation, housing, and transportation.

### Education

Education is a vital human service for the local community that includes elementary and secondary schools, colleges, universities, training centers and programs, libraries, museums, and historic landmarks. Each educational agency provides opportunities for personal growth and development to improve the quality of life in the local community. The access, availability, and quality of education resources in the local community influence the general quality of life for residents.

### Food Services

Most community residents have access to food from multiple sources, including grocery stores, convenience stores, health food stores, farmers' markets, restaurants, fast-food dispensaries, street vendors, and private and public gardens. Often in urban areas, there are challenges in access to high-quality fresh fruits and vegetables. This results from limited income, lack of transportation, and the quality of food available in local supermarkets. Community gardens are a response to this situation, but do not serve all residents in need of fresh fruits and vegetables.

The U.S. Department of Agriculture (USDA), Economic Research Service, estimated that 12.3% of households (15.6 million people) were food-insecure in 2016 (Coleman-Jensen, Rabbit, Gregory, & Sigh, 2017). Food insecurity occurs when limited access or availability disrupts the usual food intake of individuals

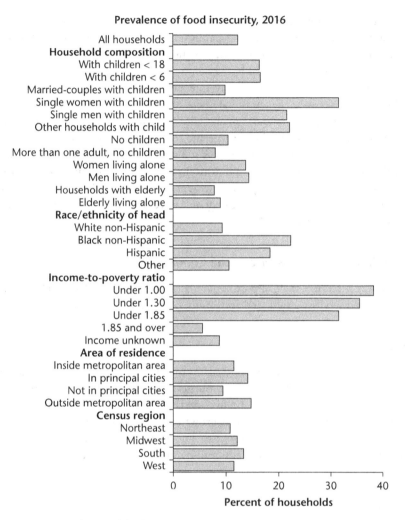

**FIGURE 3.3**  Prevalence of food insecurity

or families (Figure 3.3). Situations of food insecurity often result in disrupting the frequency of meals or compromising the nutritional value in the diet. Food insecurity most often occurs in urban, rural, and low-income communities, increased by low wages and inadequate transportation (Coleman-Jensen et al., 2017). Sources of food for individuals and families experiencing food insecurity include participating in federal food assistance programs, community food pantries, and school lunch programs for children. The USDA provides resources to each state for the Emergency Food Assistance Program. Information on how to access this resource in each state is on the website www.fns.usda.gov/fdd/food-distribution-contacts.

School lunch programs are particularly important and may be the best source of nutrition for children experiencing food insecurity. Data from the U.S. Department of Agriculture, Economic Research Service, show that in 2015, 16.6% of households with children were food-insecure (Ralston, Treen, Coleman-Jensen, & Guthrie, 2017). Among families living below the poverty line, 44% experienced food insecurity, and 23% of those experiencing food insecurity were children. The Healthy Hunger-Free Kids Act of 2010 (Pub. L. 111-296) reauthorized funding for child nutrition. Under this reauthorization, food services expanded to include after-school suppers in all 50 states, universal free meals under the National School Lunch Program and School Breakfast Program for schools in high-poverty areas, the Summer Food Service Program, and the Child and Adult Care Food Program. The nutritional value of federally supported meals for children and families is important. These programs increase food security for millions of children across the nation, especially those in urban, rural, and low-income communities (Ralston et al., 2017).

School administrators and teachers are responsible for ensuring the quality and nutritional value of food provided for students at school, and for incorporating knowledge about diet and nutrition in the school curriculum (Zimmerman, Wolf, & Haley, 2015). Including basic information about food values (calories, sodium, sugar, vitamins) with the daily or weekly menu will encourage students in making healthy food choices. Featuring and describing foods on the menu with high nutritional value increases students' knowledge for making healthy food choices. Introducing careers associated with food management and food services presents students with options for the future. Engaging students in learning experiences with community gardens and community beautification projects makes learning meaningful and encourages responsible participation in the community (Barton, 2003).

## Healthcare and Recreation

Many factors affect health conditions in a community, including access to healthcare facilities and services. The recent controversy concerning the Affordable Care Act (Obamacare) concerns issues of equitable access to healthcare for all citizens of the United States. The Affordable Care Act (ACA) aimed to expand insurance coverage that enables access to the healthcare system for low-income families and individuals. Many middle-income, wealthy, and healthy young people complained that under the ACA, their premiums increased, they were often unable to keep their primary care physician, and they paid for services they did not need in order to subsidize insurance for low-income families and individuals. Advocates for the ACA argued that the cost of caring for uninsured people who use emergency rooms as their primary source of healthcare, as well as the neglect of curable and controllable conditions, significantly increase the cost of healthcare for everybody.

Across the United States, there are significant disparities in access to health insurance and the healthcare system based on income and race. In 2016, 23.8% of poor adults were uninsured as compared to 7.8% of adults who were not poor. The percentage of people aged 18–64 not covered by insurance based on race was White (8.9%), African American (14.6%), and Latino (25.9%) (Agency for Healthcare Research and Quality, 2017).

Healthcare services are available through the federal, state, county, and municipal government. Government-sponsored healthcare services vary in administration, availability, cost, and quality. Some government-sponsored healthcare services require specific qualifications for access, such as income, specific health challenges, or affiliation with the military.

School employees need to be aware of local healthcare facilities and requirements for access in order to advise students and to locate emergency services when needed. Some government agencies provide lists, brochures, and booklets that describe local healthcare services. Making healthcare information available helps ensure that students have the knowledge necessary for access.

Recreation is an important aspect of a healthy lifestyle. The availability, access, use, and quality of recreation facilities available in a community influence the general quality of life, including physical health, mental health, community attachment, and economic security. Parks and green spaces are associated with physical activity levels, cardiovascular health, psychological health, cognitive development, and learning outcomes for children and youth (Larson, Jennings, & Cloutier, 2016).

## Housing

Urban housing types and living arrangements vary within cities and regions across the United States in architectural design, quality, and affordability. Types of housing include brick buildings, high-rise buildings, condominiums, single-family houses, and homeless shelters. Communities vary in the architectural design, quality, access, and affordability of housing. Many urban communities have a long history that is reflected in the architectural design of housing facilities, such as bungalows, craftsman, mission revival, row houses, tenements, and public housing (www.antiquehomestyle.com).

Affordable housing for low-income residents is a challenge in cities across the United States. In most cities, it is difficult to pay state and federal income tax, rent a two-bedroom single-family home or apartment, pay utilities, and buy food and other personal necessities on an income of $10 per hour or less. The median income in the United States in 2016 was $57,230. The threshold for poverty was an annual income of $26,104. In 2016, 40.6 million people across the United States lived in poverty. In 2014, 7 million people were living with family and friends, a situation often preceding homelessness. In January 2015, 564,708 people across the United States were experiencing homelessness. In 2016, 687,000 children experienced foster care.

The federal government administers, and state governments and local communities provide resources for individuals and families that need housing. Programs supported by the U.S. Department of Housing and Urban Development (www. hud.gov) include housing vouchers, rent subsidies, public housing, affordable housing for purchase, and homeless shelters. Each city or municipality has a housing authority that administers programs supported by the U.S. Department of Housing and Urban Development.

Schools are community resources for information. Making emergency housing information available at the school and ensuring that employees and students are knowledgeable encourages the use of such resources. This is important for keeping children safe and with temporary emergency shelter when needed.

Information about housing can be included across the curriculum. For example, information about the architecture and history of housing can be included in the school social studies curriculum. There are multiple opportunities for the application of mathematics in studying patterns in the design of houses and other living units, patterns in the cost of housing including mortgage loans, and demographic shifts in the population.

## Transportation

Not all community resources are located within the local neighborhood or within walking distance of every residence. Many people depend on public transportation for work, shopping, and to access other local services. The local transportation authority provides information on access to the different forms of local transportation available, and conditions and issues that influence availability and quality. Residents using personal vehicles need well-maintained and safe bridges, highways, roads, and streets.

## Application to Practice

Teaching from the center incorporates into the curriculum and pedagogical practices deep knowledge about students, including societal factors influencing their growth and development, ancestral influences on their cognitive processes, and contemporary cultural practices and community context that form their socialization. The presentation of subject matter builds upon and extends what students know and can do. Students' everyday experiences at home and in the local community serve as learning experiences. Language, culture, and experience are the essential tools in the examples that follow.

The language experience approach to early literacy learning is an example of combining children's everyday experience with language into a pedagogical tool for learning to read. In this approach, children—individually or as a group—dictate a description of an experience or construct a story transcribed by a more advanced learner or an adult. The children observe as the scribe records verbatim what the child dictates. The children read aloud the completed transcription. In this example, the children's language is the text for learning to read. Children extend their knowledge and personal experience in learning to read written text.

Lee (1995) used everyday language in a different way to teach a group of African American high school students how to interpret complex literary text. Lee used text with an African American discourse practice familiar to the students, referred to as signifying. Signifying is a verbal one-upmanship that usually incorporates figurative speech. Students learned to identify and interpret figurative speech in their own language in a way that was transferable to interpreting other complex literary text.

Brown and Ryoo (2008) described an experimental study that examined an approach to teaching science in the elementary grades with a focus on learning the content using everyday language before learning the scientific language. In this study, the control group was comprised of a randomly assigned culturally and linguistically diverse group of students. The control group learned the concept of photosynthesis using both everyday language and scientific language. When scientific terms were introduced, explanations using everyday language were discontinued. Students in the treatment group learned the concepts using everyday language without reference to scientific language. These students learned the relationship between everyday language and scientific language after they understood the concept. The students in the treatment group outperformed those in the control group on all aspects of the assessment.

Moses, Kamii, Swapp, and Howard (1989) used the students' language and experience in teaching algebra for underserved middle school students. First, teachers identified those mathematics concepts that the students found most challenging. Then a five-step approach supported the students' learning. When teaching students in a group, an experience (physical event) shared among teachers and students made explanations of concepts and the supporting thought processes visible to the group. A model or picture of the event created a visual representation for manipulating and demonstrating the concept. The students used their everyday language to describe the relationship between the event and the mathematical concept. The students revised the statement from their everyday language to the formal language of mathematics. Finally, the students convert mathematical language to mathematical symbols. This combination of experience and language proved tremendously effective in teaching students who were struggling with learning algebra.

These studies demonstrate the value of using students' home language and familiar experiences in teaching and learning in core academic subjects across grade levels. Using the home language and familiar or shared experiences is especially important when students face challenges with understanding concepts and developing skills.

## Chapter Summary

Teaching from the center is an approach that incorporates into the curriculum and pedagogy deep knowledge about students, including their ancestral knowledge, and the cultural and community context in which their socialization occurs. The curriculum and pedagogy incorporate students' ancestral knowledge (subject matter and cognitive processes) and local cultural and community context (contextualized subject matter and skills). A philosophical stance and a theoretical perspective are the foundation for teaching from the center. The philosophical stance ensures purposefulness in the curriculum and pedagogy. The theoretical perspective ensures the consistent application of particular principles of learning.

This chapter has four interrelated themes: (a) contextualizing child and adolescent growth and development; (b) framing curriculum for urban students; (c) providing equitable access to classroom learning; and (d) utilizing the community as context and text for learning. The interconnectedness of these four themes forms the core for teaching from the center. The discussion on child and adolescent growth and development addresses the challenges and complexity in the socialization of children of color in a racialized society. Framing the curriculum to support children in developing a positive ethnic and racial identity is essential for those socialized in a racialized society. Providing equitable access to classroom learning for traditionally underserved students requires using both Western analytical and non-Western holistic cognitive processes. Utilizing the community as context and text for learning actualizes purpose and meaning, deepens understanding, and contributes to the desired outcomes for students and the community in the present and future.

## References

Agency for Healthcare Research and Quality (2017, October). *National healthcare quality and disparities report 2016.* Rockville, MD: Agency for Healthcare Research and Quality.

Barton, A. C. (2003). Kobbe's story: Doing science as contested terrain. *International Journal of Qualitative Studies in Education*, 16(4), 533–552.

Beim, A. (2007). The cognitive aspects of collective memory. *Symbolic Interaction*, 30(1), 7–26.

Brown, B. A. & Ryoo, K. (2008). Teaching science as a language: A "content-first" approach to science teaching. *Journal of Research in Science Teaching*, 45(5), 529–553.

Castellano, M. B. (2000). Updating aboriginal traditions of knowledge. In G. Dei, B. Hall, & D. Rosenberg (Eds.), *Indigenous knowledges in global contexts* (pp. 23–24). Toronto: University of Toronto Press.

Coleman-Jensen, A., Rabbit, M. P., Gregory, C. A., & Sigh, A. (2017). *Household food insecurity in the United States in 2016.* Washington, DC: U.S. Department of Agriculture, Economic Research Service.

DeCuir-Gunby, J. T. (2009). A review of the identity development of African American adolescents: The role of education. *Review of Educational Research*, 79(1), 103–124.

DiMaggio, P. & Markus, H. R. (2010). Culture and social psychology: Converging perspectives. *Social Psychology Quarterly*, 73(4), 347–352.

Garcia Coll, C., Gontran, L., Jenkins, R., McAdoo, H. P., Crnic, K., Wasik, B. H., & Garcia, H. V. (1996). An integrative model for the study of developmental competencies in minority children. *Child Development*, 67, 1891–1914.

Harper, B. E. (2007). The relationship between Black racial identity and academic achievement in urban settings. *Theory into Practice*, 46(3), 230–238.

Larson, L. R., Jennings, V., & Cloutier, S. A. (2016). Public parks and wellbeing in urban areas of the United States. *PLoS ONE*, 11(4), e0153211. doi:10.137/journal.pone.0153211.

Lee, C. D. (1995). A culturally based cognitive apprenticeship: Teaching African American high school students skills in literary interpretation. *Reading Research Quarterly*, 30(4), 608–630.

Lewis, A. E. (2001). There is no "race" in the schoolyard: Color-blind ideology in an (almost) all-White school. *American Educational Research Journal*, 38(4), 781–811.

Lewis, A. E. (2003). *Race in the schoolyard: Negotiating the color line in classrooms and communities*. Piscataway, NJ: Rutgers University Press.

Li, T. M. (2000). Locating indigenous environmental knowledge in Indonesia. In R. Ellen, P. Parkes, & A. Bicker (Eds.), *Indigenous Environmental Knowledge and its Transformation* (pp. 121–150). Australia: Harwood Academic Publishers.

Mabit, J. (2002). Blending traditions: Using indigenous medicinal knowledge to treat drug addiction. *MAPS*, 12(2), 25–32.

McGregor, D. (2004). Indigenous knowledge, environment and our future. *American Indian Quarterly*, 28(3/4), 385–410.

Moje, E. B. (2007). Developing socially just subject-matter instruction: A review of the literature on disciplinary literacy teaching. *Review of Research in Education*, 31, 1–44.

Moses, R. P., Kamii, M., Swapp, S. M., & Howard, J. (1989). The algebra project: Organizing in the spirit of Ella. *Harvard Educational Review*, 59(4), 423–443.

New Teacher Project (2012). *The irreplaceables: Understanding the real retention crisis in America's urban schools*. New York: New Teacher Project.

Purcell, T. (1998). Indigenous knowledge and applied anthropology: Questions of definition and direction. *Human Organization*, 57(3), 258–272.

Ralston, K., Treen, K., Coleman-Jensen, A., & Guthrie, J. (2017). *Children's food insecurity and USDA child nutrition programs*, Washington, DC: U.S. Department of Agriculture, Economic Research Service.

Schuttenberg, H. Z. & Guth, H. K. (2015). Seeking our shared knowledge: A framework for understanding knowledge coproduction and coproductive capacities. *Ecology and Society*, 20(1), 15.

Sillitoe, P. (1998). The development of indigenous knowledge: A new applied anthropology. *Current Anthropology*, 39(2), 223–252.

Tomasello, M. (1999). *The cultural origins of human cognition*. Cambridge, MA: Harvard University Press.

U.S. Department of Education, Office of Civil Rights (2014). *Civil rights data collection. Data snapshot: School discipline*. Washington, DC: Author.

U.S. Department of Labor, Bureau of Labor Statistics (2017). *Current population survey: Unemployment rates and earnings by educational attainment, 2016*. Washington, DC: Author.

Van Ausdale, D. & Feagin, J. R. (2001). *The first R: How children learn race and racism.* Lanhan, MD: Rowman & Littlefield.

Varnum, M. E. W., Grossmann, I., Kitayama, S., & Nisbett, R. E. (2010). The origin of cultural differences: The social orientation hypothesis. *Current Directions in Psychological Sciences,* 19(1), 9–13.

Wentzel, K. R. (1991). Relations between social competence and academic achievement in early adolescence. *Child Development,* 62(5), 1066–1078.

Yip, T., Sellers, R. M., & Seaton, E. K. (2006). African American racial identity across the lifespan: Identity status, identity content, and depressive symptoms. *Child Development,* 77(5), 1504–1517.

Zimmerman, E. B., Wolf, S. H., & Haley, A. (2015). *Understanding the relationship between education and health: A review of the evidence and an examination of community perspectives.* Rockville, MD: Agency for Healthcare Research and Quality, U.S. Department of Health and Human Services. Retrieved from www.ahrq.gov/professionals/education/curriculum-tools/population-health/zimmerman.html.

# 4

# TEACHING FOR UNITY

## Focus Questions

1. How and to what extent are schools responsible for socializing students for active and amiable participation in a democratic society?
2. What is the relationship among students' social skills development, academic performance, and the social context in classrooms and schools?

## Introduction

In the present chapter, teaching for unity addresses the core skills and practices that enable living, learning, and working together in harmony with solidarity in collectively promoting the shared values of diversity, equity, freedom, and justice in a democratic society. Further, teaching for unity addresses the whole person academically, psychologically, and socially in supporting learners to reach their highest potential in all areas of the school curriculum and personal life. Teaching for unity is an approach to building relationships among people that promote solidarity in common interests, effort, and outcomes.

A central purpose for schooling is promoting the growth and development of children and youth for amiable experiences in the present while preparing for a satisfying adult life that includes meaningful contributions and active participation in a democratic society. The imperative outcome for schooling is ensuring that every student develops essential academic competence that supports continuous lifelong learning and the essential social skills necessary for participating in a democratic society. Teaching for unity engages learners in shared experiences with mutual and reciprocal benefit in developing knowledge, skills, and talents that enable each to reach her or his highest potential.

## Developing Essential Social Skills for Learning and Living

Teaching for unity requires giving careful attention to students' social and emotional development. The ability to live, learn, and work cooperatively and collaboratively within and outside of school requires clearly identifiable skills and virtues. Integrating the essential social skills across the curriculum at every grade level and subject area ensures that every student has an opportunity for learning these skills. Many approaches to developing social skills, social-emotional intelligence, and character education are interventions for students lacking specific skills for interacting in social situations. This does not ensure that every student has an opportunity to fully develop these skills. Teaching essential social skills includes attention to the core values of the society, and culturally appropriate ways of behaving and interacting in various social settings (Table 4.1). Social skills competence is essential for positioning oneself as an active and contributing participant in the society. Ensuring that every child develops appropriate social skills is part of maintaining an equitable and just society. Important skills related to social interaction and developing positive relationships with others include cognizance, communication, collaboration, and congeniality. Other skills related to social participation include compliance, respect, and responsibility.

Including social skills in the curriculum supports development of the competencies and values necessary for building positive relationships with family and friends, with peers in school, working with colleagues, and participating in and contributing to the quality of life in a democratic society. Social skills influence how we live, love, and work together with partners, in families, in social groups, and as members of a civil society. The classroom and school contexts provide many opportunities for observing students' progress in developing social skills and for providing guidance and interventions when appropriate.

The social context in schools results from the relationship between teachers and students and among students. Research shows that students who have well-developed social skills and social-emotional competence more often have positive relationships with their peers and teachers and display a more positive attitude toward school than their peers who have not developed such skills and competence. Research shows that interpersonal skills, including the ability to interact

**TABLE 4.1** Essential social skills

| Cognizance | Communication | Collaboration | Congeniality |
|---|---|---|---|
| Compliance | Appropriateness | Participation | Acceptance |
| Deference | Attentiveness | Coordination | Compromise |
| Obedience | Clarity | Flexibility | Negotiation |
| Respect | Perspective | Benevolence | Responsibility |

**TABLE 4.2** Basic attributes and virtues

| Virtues | Attributes |
| --- | --- |
| Cleanliness | Orderliness, organization, purity |
| Compassion | Caring, kindness, understanding |
| Confidence | Assertiveness, courage |
| Dignity | Honor, respect, self-control |
| Friendliness | Helpfulness, kindness, tactfulness |
| Graciousness | Polite, respectful, tactful |
| Honesty | Integrity, trustworthiness, truthfulness |
| Humility | Modesty, reserve |
| Patience | Considerate, tolerance |
| Persistence | Commitment, determination, resilience |
| Solidarity | Commitment to community interests |

effectively with peers and authority, influence academic success in school and adult socioeconomic outcomes (Jennings & DiPrete, 2010). Students with under-developed social competence often experience alienation and exclusion from their peers and do not feel supported by their teachers. Students who have antagonistic or contentious relationships with their peers are at risk for school failure, inappropriate behavior, suspension, expulsion, and for dropping out of high school due to anxiety, stress, and trauma experienced in school.

The dominant educational regime in schools across the United States is the enactment of normative codes of civility that place students in a subordinate position to adult school practitioners. Teachers and administrators control and punish students for violating behavior codes. However, the school curriculum does not routinely incorporate instruction related to the behavior codes or the related values, virtues, and character attributes (Table 4.2). Adults do not consistently model these important values. Many urban students do not routinely read or study the policy handbooks that contain the behavior codes, nor do they learn the social skills and values that support such expectations. The lack of specific knowledge about school behavior codes leaves students to act on their own perception and understanding, which often conflicts with that of school practitioners. Thus, the relationships in urban schools are often characterized by conflict and struggles for respect between school practitioners and students and among students (Hemmings, 2003).

The need for social skills development in the curriculum of urban schools is apparent in the alienation, conflict, and hostility between school practitioners and students and among students. Further evidence of the dysfunction in the social context of many urban schools is in the disproportionately high rates of suspension, expulsion, and referrals to law enforcement for ethnic minority students and students with disabilities. For example, data from the U.S. Department of Education,

Office of Civil Rights (2014) show that the rate of out-of-school suspensions for White students was 4.6% as compared to 20% for African American boys and 12% for African American girls. The out-of-school suspension rate for Hispanic/ Latino boys was 13% and 7% for girls. Common reasons for suspensions, expulsions, and referrals to law enforcement include repeated instances of disobedience, disrespect, disruptive behavior, and fighting. In addition to the apparent racial bias, these behaviors reflect students' social skills competence. The failure of many urban schools in addressing students' social development contributes to the cycle of disruption, crime, and violence in urban communities. Further, social skills development is an important factor influencing educational attainment and adult income.

The harsh discipline practices in many urban schools exacerbate the conditions for children and youth who already experience emotional distress in their daily lives within and outside of school (Noguera, 2003). A policy statement from the U.S. Department of Health and Human Services (2016) points out that: "Not only do these practices have the potential to hinder social-emotional and behavioral development, they also remove children from early learning environments and the corresponding cognitively enriching experiences that contribute to healthy development and academic success later in life" (p. 3). Further, the suspension and expulsion of children at any point in the school experience has a potential for long-term effect on their future educational attainment, social adjustment in school and life, and on their mental and physical health. Harsh punishment results in some children developing strategies for avoiding punishment that may include fear, intimidation, withdrawal, and deceptive and dishonest behavior. However, harsh punishment seldom results in children learning the social skills and cultural competence needed for success in school and life.

It is important for social skills to be developed through planned classroom experiences and specific perspectives emphasized in the subject matter of the regular curriculum. Incorporating the essential skills in Table 4.1 into the regular curriculum and daily routines in the classroom supports students' social development. Carefully designed learning experiences that require collaboration and teamwork provide opportunities for supporting skills related to social interaction and cooperation. Subject matter in English language arts, science, and social studies provide opportunities for examining character traits such as accountability, integrity, responsibility, and trustworthiness. Reminding students of the specific social skills expected during small group work reinforces practice. Acknowledging examples of specific skills and character traits in historical figures, characters in stories students read, and in students' everyday behavior provides regular support for social development. Incorporating social skills into learning experiences, integrated across the curriculum, acknowledged in students' classroom behavior, and modeled by the teacher, ensures that all students can develop socially without separate interventions or embarrassment.

In a culturally diverse society, social skills and cultural competence enable individual, within, and across group knowledge sharing, knowledge co-construction, and collaboration. Social skills are the accepted culturally appropriate ways of behaving and interacting in various social settings within a cultural group. Behaviors and ways of interacting in one culture may not be appropriate in another culture. Basic cultural competence is recognition and respect for differences in cultural and experiential backgrounds that influence behaviors, perspectives, and values, and the ability to respond in ways that are acceptable by those different from one's self. Instrumental cultural competence extends the basic competence to include knowledge of the history, language, values, and practices of different cultural groups to support cross-cultural and cross-national interactions, knowledge sharing, and collaboration. The development of social skills and cultural competence is essential for peace and prosperity in the nation and the world.

Social skills derive from specific cultures and vary across cultural groups and societies. In social skills development, cognizance is cultural and contextual knowledge of protocols for self-management, self-presentation, and social interaction and participation. It is important that the representation of social skills in the curriculum extends beyond being polite and using culture-specific "good manners" to include what is applicable within and across ethnic and cultural groups. The essential social skills applicable across ethnic and cultural groups included in this conceptualization are cognizance, communication, collaboration, and congeniality. The following discussion describes the categories and components in this conceptualization of social skills in the curriculum for elementary and secondary schools.

## Cognizance

The first category of social skills is cognizance, which refers to knowledge, mindfulness, and application of the four categories of social skills and the four components of each. The four interrelated and interdependent components of cognizance are compliance, deference, obedience, and respect.

Compliance requires knowing, accepting, and following socially accepted, policy-endorsed, and legally sanctioned standards for behavior, except in cases that threaten the well-being of self or others. Students need to know that classroom and school safety and order require that everyone comply with established rules and policies. An important aspect of social skills development is teaching students about district and school policies and regulations, especially those related to harsh discipline that impact children beginning in preschool, such as suspension, expulsion, referrals to law enforcement, and law-related arrests. Students in middle and high schools need to be familiar with "status offenses" such as truancy and underage use of alcohol that can result in referral to juvenile detention.

Establishing purpose, order, and safety whenever groups assemble, or people work together for an agency or organization, requires leadership. Leadership depends on members of the assembled group complying with the principle of deference. The principle of deference includes compliance, obedience, and respect. The principle of deference requires compliance with established policies and procedures, obedience to commands and requests, and acknowledging and supporting the authority of leaders. Students need to understand the responsibility of leaders for acting in the best interest of individuals and the collective interest of the group. Leadership responsibility includes gathering information that supports acting in the best interest of the group. When group members do not comply with the principle of deference, the group risks not achieving its purpose, disorder, or an unsafe environment. For example, when several students fail to comply with the principle of deference by disrespecting the teacher, the learning goals and safety of individuals and the group are threatened.

Obedience includes compliance with the directions and requests of those with authority or leadership; laws, policies, and regulations that govern social interaction; and participation that enables diverse populations to live together in harmony and safety. Individuals who violate the expectations for social governance pose a threat to harmony and safety for the entire population. Students need to understand the legal and ethical responsibilities of school personnel, as well as their own legal rights and liabilities, and those of their parents or guardians. Further examples of the risks associated with disobedience are hypothetical situations, including natural disasters, school shootings, and other emergency circumstances.

Respect for self and others incorporates all aspects of cognizance. Respect for one's self means protecting and accepting responsibility for one's own well-being, interests, and reputation in the present and future. Respect for self includes pride in representation and reverence for one's own culture, heritage, and family lineage. Respect for others means being considerate and mindful of the rights and responsibilities of others by providing assistance and support when needed, complying with laws, policies, and regulations, and maintaining appropriate personal boundaries.

## Communication

Communication is a process of discourse and social interaction using a common language with shared meaning. Communication entails appropriateness, attentiveness, clarity, and perspective. Communication is interrelated with the other three aspects of social skills. It is interrelated with cognizance in that appropriateness and clarity in communication require knowledge of socially accepted protocols. Collaboration requires clarity in communication and attentiveness to the ideas and perspectives presented by others. Congeniality requires appropriateness and clarity for engaging in compromise and negotiation.

Appropriateness in communication means suitable for the context or situation, includes behavior and language, and frames all discourse and social interaction. Appropriateness in behavior includes compliance, deference, obedience, and respect. Collaboration requires appropriateness in participation, coordination of action and ideas, flexibility, and benevolence. Congeniality requires appropriateness in accepting responsibility, compromise, and negotiation.

Effective communication requires attentiveness for listening, speaking, and processing information. Knowledge of the speaker and members of the audience includes culture, language, social context, and appropriate protocols supporting comprehension in communication. Attentiveness includes focused observations of the responses of the audience and speakers.

Communication involves the sharing of ideas and information. Clarity in communication among individuals and groups is essential for collaboration aimed at achieving mutually valued outcomes. Communicating with clarity requires that ideas are well-organized, coherent, and comprehensible.

Culture, socialization, experience, and education influence how individuals make sense of the world. These influences frame the interpretation of messages received through communication with others. Thus, two individuals hear the same message through different perspectives. Individuals interpret the same event through different perspectives. Deliberate perspective-taking is an important aspect of communication. Understanding different perspectives is equally important.

## Collaboration

Collaboration requires individuals to cooperate and actively participate when sharing knowledge and resources in a combined effort to address a common concern or to complete a project. The process of collaboration requires competence in the other three categories of social skills—cognizance, communication, and congeniality. Four interrelated parts of collaboration are participation, coordination, organization, flexibility, and benevolence. Contributing to a joint effort through personal knowledge and resources is a form of participation.

Collaboration requires coordination and organization of effort for sharing ideas, resources, and responsibilities. In the process of collaboration, team members identify common interests, objectives, and outcomes, and assign responsibilities and tasks. In sharing ideas, participants learn to find common ground and identify new directions by analyzing, confirming, and disconfirming evidence for supporting decision-making. Further, coordination and organization include complementary tasks distributed among team members.

Collaboration requires flexibility among team members in modifying practices that accommodate changes in internal and external circumstances and conditions related to completing specific tasks and accomplishing the desired outcomes. Flexibility includes individual and team willingness to redirect efforts or to take on additional or new responsibilities.

Benevolence is that aspect of collaboration aimed at supporting others in feeling accepted and comfortable. Benevolence includes sincere efforts in understanding others; responding to others with kindness and thoughtfulness;

demonstrating attentiveness, caring, and compassion; and offering sincere apologies or expressions of regret when others display negative emotions in responding to a situation or event.

## Congeniality

Our attitudes, dispositions, and perspectives influence the quality of our personal life and the lives of family, friends, and associates who interact with us. We have a positive effect on our own life and that of others when we display congeniality. Congeniality includes being agreeable, hopeful, pleasant, and positive. Congeniality has four components that include acceptance, compromise, negotiation, and responsibility.

Acceptance of differences in people, perspectives, and practices is an essential aspect of congeniality that enables living and working together in harmony with others. Congeniality includes acceptance of the authority and responsibilities of others, and compliance with laws, policies, rules, and regulations. Further, congeniality means identifying the appropriate approaches to change or accepting what you do not have the authority to change.

Living and working together with others requires flexibility that often entails compromise. Compromise is a process of making adjustments that accommodate others, facilitate the completion of a project, or support accomplishing a specific outcome. Compromise supports solidarity with others in addressing common interests, objectives, and outcomes.

Negotiation is an approach to considering and relinquishing competing ideas, interests, and values in the process of reaching agreement, facilitating the completion of a project, or accomplishing a specific outcome. The process of negotiation represents fairness and integrity in examining differences among ideas, interests, and values in accomplishing a satisfactory outcome for all participants.

Social arrangements in daily life with family, friends, and associates require that all participants assume responsibility related to specific roles and duties. Assuming responsibility means making a commitment to being accountable for quality, dependability, and trustworthiness of one's own performance.

## Developing Feelings of Belongingness and Connectedness

In addition to developing social skills, many children and youth need support in developing relationships with peers and adults. Early experiences within and outside of school influence how children develop relationships with peers and adults. Many children's experiences leave them feeling alienated and isolated. An important part of teaching for unity is ensuring that every student feels a sense of belongingness, connectedness, and identity with peers, the community, and the school. The sense of belongingness, connectedness, and identity derives from everyday experiences within and outside of school, and from interaction with participants in the schooling process. In this discussion, school connectedness refers to students' active engagement and identification with the school beyond and including individual subject matter, classrooms, and relationships with peers and teachers. School connectedness includes feelings of pride in the history of the school, its reputation, and recent accomplishments. Connectedness includes association with the school through extracurricular activities, including sports, music participation, clubs, and other activities. School connectedness includes feelings of belongingness associated with personal relationships among peers, teachers, and other school personnel. Feelings of connectedness and belongingness contribute to commitment and motivation to meet institutional expectations and those held by peers, teachers, and other school personnel. Developing school connectedness and belongingness requires teaching and learning practices grounded in building relationships with and among students through academic and social engagement.

In a review of the literature, Osterman (2000) found agreement among several researchers that when students experience belongingness or acceptance, they demonstrate greater intrinsic motivation, acceptance of authority, personal agency, self-regulation and responsibility, and a stronger sense of identity. Further, students experiencing belongingness demonstrate positive attitudes toward school, class assignments, peers, and teachers. Osterman (2000) concluded that:

> What this small group of studies shows is that when children experience belongingness or acceptance, their perceptions differ in predictable ways and these perceptions are associated with psychological differences. When children experience positive involvement with others, they are more likely to demonstrate intrinsic motivation, to accept the authority of others while at the same time establishing a strong sense of identity, experiencing their own sense of autonomy, and accepting responsibility to regulate their own behavior in the classroom consistent with social norms.
>
> *(p. 331)*

Children begin feeling connected to school as early as kindergarten or even in preschool. Young children's feelings about school result from relationships with peers, teachers, other adults at the school, and learning experiences. Many children do not enter school knowing the rituals, routines, and rules of engagement. In preschool and kindergarten, children learn to follow the teacher's instruction, to share, take turns, and help each other. They learn to be kind and polite. Some children need more guidance and modeling than others for learning the rules of engagement in school. Careful observations and early intervention, such as including social skills in the school curriculum, help avoid disruptions, causing children to feel embarrassed or punished when addressing individual differences in learning needs.

Urban, ethnic minority, and low-income children often experience bias and discrimination when faced with strict school district policies and harsh discipline practices. Data from the U.S. Department of Education, Institute of Education Sciences (2017) show that in 2015, a higher overall percentage of Black students (3.0%) and Hispanic students (2.9%) as compared to White students (1.8%) repeated the same grade for a second year in kindergarten through twelfth grade. The school suspension and expulsion rate for Black students is three times greater than for White students (U.S. Department of Education, Institute of Education Sciences, 2017). The cumulative effect of disparities in school discipline practices is alienation, frustration, distrust, disengagement, and disrespect for school practitioners.

Developing classrooms and schools where children and adolescents feel a sense of belongingness and connectedness requires addressing factors of guidance and support, relationships, opportunities, engagement, and outcomes. Collectively, the first four factors determine outcomes. In turn, outcomes are a measure of the

**TABLE 4.3** Challenge to retention

| |
|---|
| This is your second year teaching kindergarten at a low-income, low-performing urban elementary school. Many children attend school for the first time in kindergarten. These children are not familiar with the routines and rules of engagement in school. They have not learned to share toys or to take turns. Some children engage in tantrums. Other children are constantly in conflict with their peers. The school district has a rigid standard for academic growth in reading and mathematics for each grade level, including kindergarten. The district policy is mandated retention for children not meeting the academic growth standards. |
| You have planned for the academic, emotional, and social development of each child in your kindergarten class, beginning with an orientation to the routines and rules of engagement in school. You have posted a series of large visuals that display the daily sequence of experiences. Children work and play in friendship pairs based on compatibility. Children learn to help each other, to share, and to take turns. Children use manipulatives, visuals, and audio supports to facilitate recognizing the alphabet, counting up to 10 objects, and identifying basic colors. Most of the children have made good progress in all areas. However, three children have not met the district standards for academic growth in recognizing the alphabet, counting up to 10 objects, and identifying basic colors. These children are at risk for retention in kindergarten for a second year. |
| You know that learning experiences are the most productive when appropriately designed and sequenced, and build upon and extend what the child knows, can do, and has experienced. When pedagogy or learning experiences fail, children do not meet learning expectations. You know that punishing children with repeating a grade when pedagogy fails is unfair and may have long-term detrimental effects. |
| Develop a plan for evaluating the appropriateness of the learning experiences you provided for the children who are not meeting district expectations for kindergarten. |

collective impact of the other four factors. Careful examination of the outcomes reveals weakness in one or more of these factors.

Strict school district policies and harsh discipline practices often disrupt students' feelings of belongingness and connectedness, and their academic and social development. Policies related to grade level academic standards that require repeating a grade in elementary and middle school when expectations are not met separate students from their age/grade cohorts and cause disruption in friendships and social development. Research shows that in elementary school, children promoted to the next grade who are not meeting grade level expectations make greater academic gains than their peers who repeat the same grade the next year (Andrew, 2014; Winters & Greene, 2012). There are greater gains for individual students from social promotion than from non-promotion (review the challenge in Table 4.3). Harsh punishment such as isolation, suspension, expulsion, and referral to law enforcement disrupt and inhibit students' academic and social development. Children in need of instruction, modeling, and guidance do not learn new behaviors or social skills from harsh punishment.

## Providing Guidance, Support, and Intergenerational Connectedness

Balancing guidance, support, and opportunities is essential for the development of the whole person (Figure 4.1). Guidance from more knowledgeable others is essential for the growth and development of learners in all areas, academic, emotional, and social. Learners need information about expectations and behaviors, contexts, and conditions. Learners need to know the purpose for specific expectations and the personal and societal consequences for not meeting expectations. For example, at the beginning of each school year, it is important to present an overview of the expectations, rules, and regulations that constitute the policies for the school and school district. Making explicit each category of expectations, and the personal and societal consequences for not meeting the expectations, ensures exposure for every student. Explicit instruction includes assigned reading or video presentations and learning experiences such as small group discussions or tasks and working through dilemmas and simulations that require making critical choices and decisions. Explicit instruction applies to all aspects of school expectations and responsibility for student growth in all areas, academic, emotional, and social. Situations from previous years involving students in failing to meet expectations or disciplinary action are good sources for working through dilemmas and simulations. The use of explicit instruction is especially important in schools that enroll a high percentage of traditionally underserved students.

Providing support for students in meeting expectations and policies goes beyond explicit instruction to include coaching, mentoring, and modeling from school practitioners and community members. The complexity of the knowledge and skills required, as well as the background knowledge and performance of

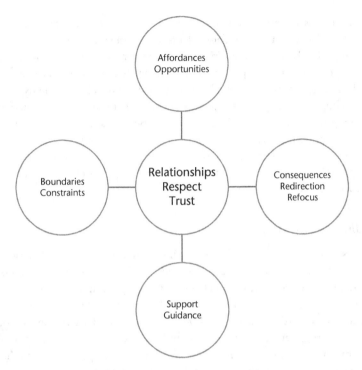

**FIGURE 4.1**  Balancing guidance, support, and opportunities

learners, determine the level of support needed for meeting expectations within the school and the community. Indicators of the need to change or increase support or practices include students not meeting expectations or repeated failure to comply with school, classroom, district, or community standards for behavior and performance. For example, the preponderance of low academic performance in a classroom or school and the repeated need for harsh disciple such as exclusion, suspension, expulsion, or referral to law enforcement indicate a need for increasing the support for students in meeting expectations or for changes in community, classroom, or school practices.

Coaching is an approach for supporting students in meeting expectations and complying with community, classroom, and school requirements. Community members can volunteer to serve as coaches in the schools and in the community. Coaching involves providing incremental instruction as needed, monitoring progress, and providing feedback. The need for incremental instruction is indicated by the questions students ask indicating gaps in knowledge or misunderstandings, observing students' behavior and performance, and formative assessments. Coaching helps students develop perspectives, and interpret and apply fundamental knowledge, procedures, and practices.

Mentoring is an approach where a more knowledgeable and trusted individual provides guidance and support for students in meeting academic and social expectations for schools and communities. The mentor models life experiences as well as the application of concepts, procedures, practices, and skills. The mentor is a good listener and encourages the learner in working to solve problems.

Modeling is an approach to supporting students in meeting expectations and complying with classroom and school requirements that involves demonstrating, illustrating, presenting, and representing concepts, procedures, practices, or skills. Modeling includes observable behaviors, practices, actions, or products completed or prepared by a more competent individual or group. Coaching, instructing, and mentoring employ modeling.

## *Building Relationships*

Students observe caring actions from school practitioners through support and guidance, the quality of opportunities made available, listening and responding to students' concerns and perspectives, expressions of appreciation and recognition for students' accomplishments, and fairness in the treatment of every student. These acts of caring displayed by adults model the expectations for students. Caring relationships among students are observable in acts of advocacy, concern, empathy, kindness, inclusion, interest, respect, responsibility, and trustworthiness. Students learn core values that support caring relationships from modeling by school practitioners and explicit instruction. Relationships among peers and between teachers and students are important contributing factors to students' feelings of belongingness and connectedness. Important characteristics of supportive relationships include caring, empathy, respect, trust, and solidarity. The extent to which these characteristics are present in the relationships among participants in a classroom or school determines the social climate, influences feelings of belongingness and connectedness, and mediates learning outcomes. The characteristics of relationships among participants are observable in everyday actions and interactions.

Intergenerational connectedness within the community is important for developing students' feelings of belongingness and connectedness within the community and school. It is important for students to recognize, celebrate, and learn from individuals who make a difference through leadership and service in the local community. Community members can provide support for the emotional and social development of students through coaching, mentoring, and modeling. Classroom teachers and schools can support intergenerational connectedness through activities such as creating a special wall at the school for *community members making a difference*. This wall can include community leaders such as city council members, members of local governing boards, and other community members making important contributions to the community. Students can develop scrapbooks of news article clippings on community members' contributions. Students can write and publish a series on *Profiles of Community Service* describing important contributions of individuals in the local community. Displaying students' work prominently in the school presents local individuals as models of participatory citizenship. Bringing local individuals who are making a difference in the community into the school to interact with students provides opportunities for mentoring and modeling.

## Providing Opportunities

Opportunities are specific conditions or situations that provide immediate availability and access to the essential and environmental factors that facilitate accomplishing a desired outcome. High-quality, meaningful, and relevant opportunities facilitate the growth and development of learners in all areas, academic, emotional, and social. The meaningfulness of an opportunity results from its relevance in connecting what the learner knows and values in applying new approaches to addressing goals, needs, or desires. The interrelatedness among purpose, substance, structure, and experience increase the quality of the opportunity and the probability for success.

Students gain awareness of opportunities through multiple sources made available by school practitioners, community members, and the media. Teachers make learning opportunities available in the classroom using explicit instruction. Teachers identify learning opportunities outside the classroom in the community. School counselors and mentors from outside the school provide opportunities for extracurricular activities and experiences beyond the classroom related to careers or higher education. Further, students may identify opportunities in the media, including the Internet. It is important to provide guidelines for evaluating opportunities.

## Active Engagement

Engagement is active participation in an activity, experience, or project with qualities that *command* the attention, commitment, and interest of the learner. Powerful experiences that command the attention and commitment of learners have purpose, meaning, and relevance, and challenge the imagination, knowledge, and skill of the learner. Meaningful experiences that capture the interest of the learner embody the values of the learner, and build upon and extend the knowledge and skill of the learner in completing a project, addressing an issue, or solving a problem. Usually, active participation in the most powerful experiences involves interacting with others in dialogue or completing a project or task (www.edutopia.org/article/junior-historians-work).

The benefits of active engagement for learners are multifaceted. Active engagement in project-based learning or problem-solving involves learners in collaboration, which develops social skills, respect for multiple perspectives, the art of compromising, and academic knowledge and skills. Learners develop confidence and self-esteem. Guidance and support from more knowledgeable others help to maintain learners' engagement in meaningful experiences.

## Meeting Expectations

The qualities of guidance and support, relationships, opportunities, and engagement provided for students influence outcomes related to academic achievement and performance. Students are more likely to meet expectations for outcomes with high-quality guidance, support, and environmental conditions. High-quality guidance, support, and environmental conditions bolster students' feelings of belongingness and connectedness in school. Guidance and support from school practitioners and peers have a significant impact on students' feelings of belongingness and connectedness. Nasir, Jones, and McLaughlin (2011) pointed out that:

> Connection is an inherently relational construct, one that involves both what a student brings to the environment (from a history of their interaction in other environments and their personal lives) and what the environment offers to support school achievement, to promote school failure and disengagement or to anticipate disconnection for the student.
>
> *(p. 1785)*

Further, Osterman (2000) pointed to research findings that link:

> the experience of relatedness or belongingness to outcomes of particular significance in educational settings: 1) the development of basic psychological processes important to student success, 2) academic attitudes and motives, 3) social and personal attitudes, 4) engagement and participation, and 5) academic achievement.
>
> *(p. 327)*

Some students need more guidance and support from school practitioners than do others because their experiences within and outside of school have been inadequate for promoting their academic, emotional, and social growth and development (Nichols, 2006).

## Developing Essential Academic Competence

Academic competence, social skills, and feelings of belongingness and connectedness are interrelated. Students who lack social skills are often excluded and isolated by their peers, perform poorly academically, and do not feel a sense of belongingness and connectedness to school. Often students who perform poorly are embarrassed and avoid interacting with peers. Competence in essential academic skills rooted in literacy development is a core challenge.

Developing academic competence is a process that begins in preschool and continues through graduate school. Basic skills for accessing and processing information received through different receptors and from multiple sources for constructing meaning are essential academic skills. Language and literacy are examples of *essential academic skills*. Discipline-specific approaches to knowledge construction, representation, reasoning, discourse, and inquiry are *instrumental academic skills* that enable the process for constructing deep knowledge within a specific discipline (Ford & Forman, 2006; Monte-Sano, 2010). Essential and instrumental academic skills support *executive function skills*, such as perception, that operate through mental processes to organize and interpret information received through different receptors and multiple sources.

## Literacy in Developing Cognitive Processes

The development of essential academic skills in literacy in the early grades supports cognitive processes that influence all subsequent learning (Herbers et al., 2012). For example, word recognition skills such as decoding, context clues, and vocabulary building help learners develop a schematic for the pronunciation of new words, attending to the meaning of individual words and examining how context influences word meaning. The cognitive process inherent in early literacy development of attending to details, recognizing patterns and relationships, is a prerequisite for subsequent learning across grade levels and subject matter areas. If the learner does not develop cognitive processes for decoding or reading comprehension, a generalized struggle with learning is likely to occur and persist across grade levels.

The representation of ideas is cultural, located within a context, framed by historical perspective, and bounded by linguistic traditions (Tatum, 2009). Reading comprehension is a complex process of meaning-making that is cultural, contextual, experiential, historical, and linguistic. It is important to point out that teaching reading through a phonics-based approach is grounded in a specific linguistic tradition and depends on the learner having developed the cognitive processes of auditory and visual discrimination. Reading comprehension requires cognitive processes of analysis, interpretation, extrapolation, summarization, and synthesis.

The cognitive processes involved in literacy development support subsequent learning, whether from written text, planned learning experiences, or formal or informal observations. Making cognitive processes explicit by identifying their component parts and interrelationships increases accessibility for learners and strengthens academic preparation for deeper learning. For example, analysis includes comparing and contrasting by identifying similarities and differences in characteristics of phenomena and identifying patterns that occur within and across units of analysis. Engaging in analysis supports generalizing, drawing conclusions, and making inferences. Generalizing, drawing conclusions, and making inferences involve summarizing and synthesizing information to form a hypothesis or proposition. Conclusions and inferences are propositions that make predictions or projections beyond that supported by evidence. Evidence based on experimentation and observation confirms or disconfirms specific propositions. In sum, analysis is the examination of relationships within and across units, which constitutes an essential cognitive process for literary, mathematical, and scientific thinking.

Specific cognitive processes learned in early literacy development, including attention to detail, recognizing patterns in relationships, making inferences, and drawing conclusions, apply across disciplines. Shanahan and Shanahan (2008) described the basic structural elements for chemistry, mathematics, and history. The authors described the basic structural elements of chemistry as substances, properties, processes and interactions, and atomic expressions. Mathematics includes operations, theorems, proofs, explanations, and illustrations (formulas, diagrams, graphs). History is an account of events that addresses who, what, when, where, how, and why, from which cause-and-effect relationships are inferred. Understanding the structural elements of a discipline gives attention to details that enable identifying patterns and making inferences that support conclusions.

Knowledge of the relationship among the structural elements representing the details of a discipline is foundational for engaging in the authentic discourse and practices of a discipline. For example, Monte-Sano (2010) describes the practices used by historians in constructing historical accounts to include: (1) factual and interpretive accuracy; (2) persuasiveness of evidence; (3) sourcing of evidence; (4) corroboration of evidence; and (5) contextualization of evidence. Factual accuracy and sourcing require attention to detail. Persuasiveness, corroboration, and contextualization require the ability to identify patterns and relationships. Further, intertextuality (comparing evidence across multiple sources) and intercontextuality (making connections among events across places and time) require a more sophisticated application of knowledge of details and patterns in providing evidence to support an argument representing a conclusion about a historical event. Drawing conclusions about a historical event requires making inferences, a cognitive process learned in early literacy development.

The cognitive processes learned during literacy acquisition and development in elementary and secondary school are essential for post-secondary education and for functioning as a competent adult in a democratic society. A long-standing purpose of education has been helping students understand the application of knowledge to practice in support of improving the quality of life in communities, the nation, and the planet. This includes the application of specific subject matter knowledge and cognitive processes. This knowledge is useful in everyday life, pursuing higher education, or in the pursuit of a career.

In middle and secondary schools, it is important to extend essential skills to incorporate the discourse, practices, and tools used by academicians and practitioners in a specific discipline. It is important for students to understand how a discipline is organized, ways of representing ideas, and methods of inquiry. At a very basic level, the cognitive processes learned in early literacy development extend across the grade levels and apply to specific subject areas. For example, practices in each discipline include attention to details, the relationship among details, patterns in the relationship among details or parts to the whole, and the application of subject matter knowledge to practice (Table 4.2).

## Application to Practice

The learning experiences in classrooms focused on teaching for unity build and incorporate essential social skills, feelings of belongingness and connectedness, and essential academic skills into collaboration and teamwork. The learning experiences are inquiry-based, problem-based, and project-based. Students form collaborative groups or teams to examine issues and problems related to: (a) environmental events, factors, and issues; (b) cultural and historical change; (c) social conditions and issues; and (d) societal and personal values and virtues. The issues and problems students study relate to the past, present, and future. These topics are located within and across subject matter areas. This collaborative inquiry approach develops unity in the form of individual and collective responsibility among students for achieving the expected outcomes.

### Collaboration, Teamwork, and Academic Engagement

Creating a climate of collaboration and teamwork in urban schools is especially important for improving academic performance, promoting cordial and congenial relationships among students and developing solidarity. Collaboration and teamwork support learning skills of negotiation based on accommodation and compromise, adaptation and adjustment. Collaboration and teamwork help students understand and value difference and diversity. Finally, collaboration and teamwork promote feelings of belongingness and connectedness that support students' emotional and social development.

Collaboration and teamwork support a social constructivist perspective on learning. In describing a constructivist perspective, De Corte (2011/2012) states that "Learners are viewed not as passively receiving information, but as actively constructing knowledge and skills through reorganisation of their previously acquired mental structures" (p. 35). This suggests that the processing of new information transforms existing knowledge through accommodation or assimilation. In assimilation, existing categories or schemas expand to incorporate new knowledge as examples or variations on existing knowledge. In accommodation, new categories or schemas develop to accommodate new knowledge that is distinct. De Corte (2011/2012) further points out that "Effective learning is a distributed activity, not a purely solitary one. The learning effort is distributed over the individual student; the partners in the learning environment; and the available resources, technology, and tools (Salomon, 1993)" (p. 36). This indicates that students learn from and with each other through participation in joint activity that supports co-constructing shared meaning and understanding.

Examples of collaborative and teamwork approaches include inquiry-based learning, problem-based learning, and project-based learning. These approaches engage learners in active, co-constructive, cumulative, self-regulated, goal-directed, situated, collaborative, and individually appropriated learning processes. Other teamwork arrangements include task assignments involving pairs, triads, or small groups of students engaged in short-term experiences focused on a process for developing understanding of a concept, principle, or skill necessary for application in a larger project, assignment, or practice supporting increasingly complex learning or performance. In some instances, a problem-based or project-based approach is carefully constructed and sequenced as task assignments. A central purpose for using inquiry-based approaches is to enable students to use the knowledge and skills learned appropriately and effectively in different contexts and for different purposes.

Curriculum alignment is an important part of the planning process for meaningful and productive learning when using inquiry-based approaches, including problem-based and project-based approaches (Peck, 2010). Curriculum alignment refers to the process of identifying the relationship among curriculum standards for elementary and secondary student learning from different sources, including state standards, common core standards, and standards for specific disciplines or from professional organizations. In the alignment process, corresponding and complementary standards positioned together and sequenced developmentally form the basis for developing specific learning objectives or learning outcomes, learning experiences, and identifying appropriate resources and tools. De Corte's (2011/2012) statement that "Learners are viewed not as passively receiving information, but as actively constructing knowledge and skills through reorganisation of their previously acquired mental structures" (p. 35) highlights the importance of curriculum alignment and sequencing, and the development of meaningful and purposeful learning experiences.

Inquiry-based learning is rich and complex in that it has depth and is multidimensional. Well-designed inquiry-based learning is purposeful and meaningful. Purposeful learning experiences teach more than carefully aligned and sequenced standards and specific learning objectives. Learning experiences address discipline-specific knowledge and practices, core societal values (equity, freedom, justice, diversity, and solidarity), and social skills supporting collaboration and teamwork. Discipline-specific knowledge includes conceptual and procedural knowledge, as well as approaches to inquiry resulting in new knowledge. Table 2.2 provides a summary of the discipline-specific purposes and practices for history and science. Incorporating discipline-specific purposes and practices into inquiry-based learning experiences supports deep knowledge and adaptive competence (De Corte, 2011/2012).

**TABLE 4.4** Thematic categories

| | |
|---|---|
| **I.** | **Environmental events, factors, and issues** |
| | a. Dust bowl, 1930s |
| | b. Valdez oil spill, 1989 |
| | c. Elk River chemical spill, 2014 |
| | d. San Francisco earthquake, 1906 |
| | e. Galveston, Texas hurricane, 1901 |
| | f. Hurricane Katrina, 2005 |
| | g. Tsunami in Puerto Rico, 1918 |
| | h. Hawaii volcano eruption, 2018 |
| | i. Detroit, Michigan water crisis, 2014 |
| **II.** | **Cultural and historical change** |
| | a. Wright brothers first flight, 1903 |
| | b. Invention of the telephone, 1876 |
| | c. Hitler becomes German chancellor, 1933 |
| | d. Industrial Revolution, 1740–1820 |
| | e. Mathematical calculator invented, 1970 |
| | f. Modern Internet launched, 1983 |
| | g. Beginning of television broadcasting, 1940s |
| | h. Hiroshima atomic bomb, 1945 |
| | i. First person to orbit the earth, 1961 |
| **III.** | **Social conditions and issue** |
| | a. Distribution of wealth, poverty, hunger, homelessness |
| | b. Citizenship, immigration |
| | c. Governance, safety, violence, incarceration |
| | d. Social justice, human rights |
| **IV.** | **Societal and personal values and virtues** |
| | a. Individualism, communalism |
| | b. Competition, teamwork, collaboration |
| | c. Empathy, kindness |
| | d. Trustworthiness, honesty |
| | e. Integrity, fairness |
| | f. Perseverance, persistence |

Table 4.4 provides examples of categories and topics for use in inquiry-based, problem-based, or project-based learning. The depth and dimensions of the categories and topics in Table 4.4 are suitable for incorporating into the core curriculum of English language arts, mathematics, science, and social studies at the elementary, middle, and high school levels. The categories are flexible and can accommodate many different topics. The topics listed in each category provide opportunities for developing many different questions, problems, and projects. These topics are suitable for developing themes that cut across subject areas. For example, in category I, environmental events, factors, and issues in English language arts, the novel *Dark Water Rising* by Marian Hale is appropriate

for middle school students. This novel is about the Galveston, Texas hurricane in 1901. When reading this novel, students can use their mathematical skills to measure and record the extent of the devastation by the hurricane. The novel *Dark Water Rising* provides meaningful context for study in meteorology related to hurricanes. Students can use primary and secondary sources not included in the novel to construct a historical narrative that contextualizes the 1901 hurricane. Reading the novel *Dark Water Rising* provides a good introduction for a project investigating, mapping, and determining the capacity of safety shelters for local natural disasters.

Collaboration and teamwork require an appropriate organizational structure. One approach is to organize the class into teams based on complementary knowledge, skills, and talents that will ensure that each member of the team contributes to completing the assignment, project, or task. The experience is designed such that each team member develops the knowledge and skills to demonstrate the highest level of performance on the project and/or the assessment of learning. Class time is used for receiving information needed for the project and time to work together with team members. Homework may consist of listening to lectures or instruction for practicing aspects of the project necessary for working together with peers. Unexpected situations can result in challenges that disrupt the best plans. Review the challenge in Table 4.3.

## Chapter Summary

The core concept framing this chapter is teaching for unity. Teaching for unity is about supporting students in learning to live and work together in harmony as a community with shared values, assuming individual and collective responsibility for advancing shared goals and outcomes. The daily practices in classrooms employing the *teaching for unity* concept include promoting the development of basic academic competence, social skills competency, feelings of belongingness and connectedness, and the ability to engage in collaboration and teamwork. Acquiring basic academic and social skills and competency prepares students for progressing through increasingly complex and demanding learning assignments and for developing relationships with peers and adults. Academic and social competence are foundational for feelings of belongingness and connectedness in school. Feelings of belongingness and connectedness increase the self-confidence and self-esteem that support academic engagement and success, as well as satisfying relationships with peers and adults. Collaboration and teamwork support deeper learning and encourage assuming individual and collective responsibility for advancing shared goals and achieving desired outcomes. Unity in assuming individual and shared responsibility for the common good is foundational for transforming urban communities.

# References

Andrew, M. (2014). The scarring effects of primary-grade retention? A study of cumulative advantage in the education career. *Social Forces*, 93(2), 653–685.

De Corte, E. (2011/2012). Constructive, self-regulated, situated, and collaborative learning: An approach for the acquisition of adaptive competence. *The Journal of Education*, 192(2/3), 33–47.

Ford, M. J. & Forman, E. A. (2006). Redefining disciplinary learning in classroom contexts. *Review of Research in Education*, 30, 1–32.

Hemmings, A. (2003). Fighting for respect in urban high schools. *Teachers College Record*, 105(3), 416–437.

Herbers, J. E., Cutuli, J. J., Suphoff, L. M., Heistad, D., Chan, C., Heinz, E., & Masten, A. S. (2012). Early reading skills and academic achievement trajectories of children facing poverty, homelessness, and high residential mobility. *Educational Researcher*, 41(9), 366–374.

Jennings, J. L. & DiPrete, T. A. (2010). Teacher effects on social and behavioral skills in early elementary school. *Sociology of Education*, 83(2), 135–159.

Monte-Sano, C. (2010). Disciplinary literacy in history: An exploration of the historical nature of adolescents' writing. *Journal of the Learning Sciences*, 19(4), 539–568.

Nasir, N. S., Jones, A., & McLaughlin, M. (2011). School connectedness for students in low-income high schools. *Teachers College Record*, 113(8), 1755–1793.

Nichols, S. L. (2006). Teachers' and students' beliefs about student belonging in one middle school. *The Elementary School Journal*, 106(3), 255–271.

Noguera, P. A. (2003). Schools, prisons, and social implications of punishment: Rethinking disciplinary practices. *Theory into Practice*, 42(4), 341–350.

Osterman, K. F. (2000). Students' need for belonging in the school community. *Review of Educational Research*, 70(3), 323–367.

Peck, S. M. (2010). Not on the same page but working together: Lessons from an award-winning urban elementary school. *The Reading Teacher*, 63(5), 394–403.

Shanahan, T. & Shanahan, C. (2008). Teaching disciplinary literacy to adolescents: Rethinking content-area literacy. *Harvard Educational Review*, 78(1), 40–59.

Tatum, A. (2009). *Reading for their life: (Re)building the textual lineage of African American adolescent males*. Princeton, NJ: Heinemann.

U.S. Department of Education, Institute of Education Sciences (2017). *Indicator 14: Retention, suspension, and expulsion*. Washington, DC: Author.

U.S. Department of Education, Office of Civil Rights (2014). *Civil rights data collection. Data snapshot: School discipline*. Washington, DC: Author.

U.S. Department of Health and Human Services (2016). *Policy statement on expulsion and suspension policies in early childhood settings*. Retrieved from www2.ed.gov/policy/gen/guid/school-discipline/policy-statement-ece-expulsions-suspensions.pdf.

Winters, M. A. & Greene, J. P. (2012). The medium-run effects of Florida's test-based promotion policy. *Education Finance and Policy*, 793, 305–330.

# 5

# TEACHING TO RESTORE

## Focus Questions

1. What factors within school contribute to stress and trauma for children, and what is the impact on classroom learning and participation?
2. How do teachers determine appropriate ways to mitigate situations and support children who regularly experience stress and trauma within and outside of school?

## Introduction

> Rather than helping youths navigate the turbulence they experience growing up in the current social order, society quickly labels young people as undesirable troublemakers and perceives them as disposable commodities.
>
> *(Pomeroy & Browning, 2010, p. 197)*

This chapter addresses teaching to restore the academic, psychological, and social well-being of children and youth who experience trauma in their lives, including alienation, isolation, rejection, abandonment, displacement, neglect, and victimization. The discussion addresses approaches to classroom support for students living with peer rejection, distracted parents, in poverty, homeless, in extended families, in foster care, group homes, incarcerated, and those who are refugees. In the United States, more than 3 million children and youth live in poverty. More than 1 million children and youth in the United States experienced at least one night in a homeless situation in 2017. Children and youth living with conditions of poverty and displacement experience unhealthy living conditions, food insecurity, inadequate medical care, social isolation, victimization, and inadequate parental support. These traumatic life conditions place children at risk for negative effects on their growth and development physically, emotionally, socially, and educationally. For many children living with trauma, school is the most safe and predictable experience in their lives. This increases the responsibility of school practitioners for being attentive and responsive to the needs of these children. However, many children and youth experience trauma both within and outside of school.

Wright and Ryan (2014) identified two types of trauma. Type I trauma consists of events that are unexpected, short-term, may have multiple causes, and some are beyond the control of single individuals, such as natural disasters resulting from earthquakes, hurricanes, tornados, or volcanoes, and accidents (dog bites, explosions, fires, motor vehicle accidents). Other traumatic experiences included in this category are violent experiences, including bombing, shooting, rape, kidnapping, robbery, and industrial accidents. Type II trauma is chronic, continuous, repeated, or long-term. Examples of type II trauma include chronic illness, child maltreatment, domestic abuse, and imprisonment. Other examples of type II trauma include bullying, exploitation, harassment, or isolation at school, and extreme poverty, homelessness, or other displacement, and the death of a loved one or pet, or a friend moving away. Wright and Ryan (2014) pointed out that "repetitive behaviors, vivid recurring memories, trauma specific fears, and negative attitudes about life and people in general are four most consistent signs of childhood trauma" (p. 88). Children with similar traumatic experiences respond differently based on the circumstances before, during, and after the experience. Some children develop symptoms that interfere with learning in school, relationships with peers and teachers, and result in inappropriate and disruptive behaviors.

The challenge teachers face is that of supporting the individual child's recovery from trauma while maintaining a comfortable and supportive social context for learning for all children. The first principle of ethical practice for teaching to restore or to support children in recovering from trauma is to do no harm. This principle requires that teachers have knowledge of their students, their needs and life experiences, their responses to the learning experiences provided, and the impact of their own action and behavior on their students. Doing no harm means avoid engaging in actions and situations that cause discomfort, embarrassment, humiliation, or stress for children, or any action that is or has the appearance of being inappropriate in relationships with children. The second principle of ethical practice for teaching to restore is always act in the best interest of students. This requires that teachers are proactive in anticipating and preventing harm to their students. The second principle requires that teachers are aware of their students' needs and act to promote their well-being in all areas, academically, physically, psychologically, and socially.

The responsibility for maintaining a safe and supportive environment in the classroom and school is a primary requirement for the first principle of ethical practice for teaching to restore, *do no harm*. This includes protecting children and youth from maltreatment by peers and school personnel. Attending school and participating in learning experiences should not cause any type of harm to students, including physical, psychological, or social. However, data from the National Center for Education Statistics (2017) indicate that in 2015, 20.8% of students aged 12–18 reported that they were victims of bullying at school. Bullying included ridicule or insult, subject of rumors, physical infraction (pushed, shoved, tripped, spit on), deliberate or hostile exclusion, threat of harm, attempted coercive action, and property destruction. Among the students who reported being the victim of bullying, 33% experienced bullying inside classrooms. Forty-one percent experienced bullying in hallways or stairwells. Among the students who experienced bullying, 19% reported that it occurred once or twice a month, 9% experienced bullying once or twice a week, and 4% experienced bullying almost every day. Bullying had a significant impact on the victim's schoolwork, relationships with friends and family, feeling about self, and physical health. Teachers need to recognize the signs of bullying and ways of preventing it. For more information and training on how to stop bullying for educators and bus drivers, go to www.stopbullying.gov. For information on how to respond to incidents of racism, bullying, and hate in schools, visit http://neatoday.org/safeschools/.

Among the most egregious offenses that occur in school at all levels, kindergarten through twelfth grade, is sexual abuse. Mitchell (2010) defines sexual abuse as:

> (a) any sexual act between an adult and a minor, or between two minors, when one exerts power over the other; and (b) forcing or persuading a child to engage in any type of sexual act. In addition to sexual contact, the definition of sexual act also includes noncontact acts such as exhibitionism, exposure to pornography, voyeurism, and communication in a sexual manner by phone or Internet.
>
> *(p. 102)*

The perpetrators of sexual offenses include same-age peers, older children victimizing younger children, and school personnel exploiting children and youth. The Associated Press conducted a yearlong investigation in which it was found that across the United States, more than 17,000 student-to-student sexual assaults were documented over a four-year period from the fall of 2011 to the spring of 2015. These data were from education records and federal crime data; however, many sexual assaults among students occurring in school go unreported (McDowell, Dunklin, Schmall, & Pritchard, 2017).

Recent data on school personnel perpetrating sexual crimes against children are not readily available. In 2004, the U.S. Department of Education commissioned a report written by Charol Shakeshaft in which it was reported that 1 in 10 students experienced sexual misconduct by school personnel during their time as students in P-12 schools. The reporting of instances of sexual misconduct by school personnel in local newspapers is all too familiar.

Walter (2018) pointed out that:

> Historically, teachers and other school employees who have committed sex-related crimes against students have not been investigated, prosecuted, or forced to face consequences for their crimes (Shakeshaft, 2004). In fact, many school personnel who have allegedly behaved in this manner moved from school to school, district to district, or across state lines when allegations were made or became known in the school or community.
>
> *(p. 2)*

The failure of school administrators to investigate and hold school personnel accountable for sexual misconduct is one reason that students are reluctant to report sexually inappropriate behavior perpetrated by school personnel. Further, teachers and administrators often accuse students of making false reports of school personnel misconduct.

Shakeshaft (2013) observed that:

> School faculty and staff often rally around a teacher accused of sexual misconduct while shunning and shaming the victim. Even when the accused admits the crime, colleagues have been charmed and groomed to such a degree that some conclude the predator confessed to spare family and friends the embarrassment of a public trial.
>
> *(p. 10)*

Such action by faculty and staff is in violation of the Child Abuse Prevention and Treatment Act (CAPTA), originally enacted in 1974, reauthorized in 2010, and amended to include the Victims of Trafficking Act of 2015 and in 2016 to include the Comprehensive Addition and Recovery Act. CAPTA, regarding the definition of child abuse and neglect, states that:

> The term "child abuse and neglect" means, at a minimum, any recent act or failure to act on the part of a parent or caretaker which results in death, serious physical or emotional harm, sexual abuse or exploitation (including sexual abuse as determined under section III), or an act or failure to act which presents an imminent risk of serious harm.
>
> *(CAPTA, 2016, section 3, p. 7)*

CAPTA provides funding to states for developing child protective services to prevent child abuse and neglect. In most states, teachers and administrators as caretakers for children are mandated reporters of suspected child abuse, neglect, and exploitation, including sexual offenses (Duger, 2015). Mandated reporting does not require that teachers or administrators investigate or provide evidence of child abuse, neglect, or exploitation. The mandate requires reasonable suspicion of the maltreatment of a child. Failure to comply with mandated reporting can result in the revocation of professional license, a fine, and/or incarceration. Educators need to be familiar with the signs and symptoms of child maltreatment. Many children and youth experience trauma within and outside of school perpetrated by peers and trusted adults. The psychological trauma these children experience can become unbearable to the extent of resulting in tragedy. The best hope for vulnerable and victimized children and youth is educators following laws for their protection and applying the principles of *do no harm* and *act in the best interest of the child*.

## Homelessness among Families and Children without Families

The basic cause of homelessness among families with children is limited financial resources. Unemployment, periodic and seasonal employment, and low-wage employment are reasons for limited financial resources. Examples of factors contributing to limited resources for parents include poor quality of education received in low-performing schools, dropping out of high school, shifts in technology that eliminate jobs and a reduction in the number of jobs available, immigration status, and catastrophic illness, death, or incarceration of the primary wage earner. Wildeman (2014) found that mass incarceration among Black men significantly increased the risk of homelessness of Black children. It is important to recognize that Black men disproportionately receive longer jail sentences for minor offences and wrongful convictions in comparison to their White counterparts. These convictions cause Black men to fail background checks, thus causing permanent unemployment.

The devastating impact of cycles of homelessness and persistent homelessness can affect multiple generations. Cutuli and Herbers (2014) pointed out that:

> In addition, parents who are homeless with their children often have experienced significant risk and adversity in their own developmental histories, including abuse and neglect, foster care placements, or homelessness as children . . . After their difficult experiences, many of these parents have untreated emotional, chemical, or behavioral problems, such as substance abuse, depression, or ongoing symptoms of post-traumatic stress . . . Furthermore, parents who are homeless often arrive at shelter after acute traumatic experiences, such as domestic violence, neighborhood violence, house fires, or other disasters . . . These risk factors tend to accumulate among parents experiencing homelessness and threaten their capacity for warm, nurturing parenting . . . Parents in homeless families often have limited economic resources, limited knowledge of typical child development, lack of experience with positive parent role models, and limited access to social support.
>
> *(pp. 125–126)*

Homelessness can be sudden and unexpected, temporary, or persistent. Accommodation for temporary homelessness includes living in shelters or with family or friends. Families experiencing persistent homelessness find accommodation in cars, abandoned buildings, in parks, and on the street.

Murphy and Tobin (2011) identified three categories of unaccompanied homeless children, runaways, throwaways, and system homeless. Runaways and throwaways leave their permanent residence because of conflicts with or abuse from adult caregivers. Runaways voluntarily leave the home. Adult caregivers forced throwaway children out of the home. The system homeless include children placed in government programs and foster care. These conditions contribute to the estrangement of children from their families.

Homeless children experience trauma inside and outside of school due to their life condition. Inside school, homeless children face many peers, teachers, and administrators with little understanding and empathy for their life conditions. Peers often exclude and ridicule homeless children. Some teachers avoid contact with homeless children, fail to support their social interactions with peers, and punish them for failing to complete homework. There are instances in which administrators suspend homeless children for being absent from school and for retaliating against ridicule from their peers without responding to the ridicule experienced. Outside of school, homeless children fear uncertainty and instability, personal safety, food insecurity, unhealthy living conditions, lack of privacy, and the inability to meet health and personal hygiene needs. For some children, the situation becomes unbearable, resulting in devastating consequences of injury to self or others.

The trauma homeless children face within and outside of school has a negative impact on their growth and development academically, psychologically, and socially. Homeless children often do not have access to resources for supporting their academic development, including a place to study and complete homework, or the necessary tools to complete assignments. Homeless children are more likely to fail classes or to repeat a grade in elementary and middle school than peers that have a permanent family residence. The cumulative stress and trauma associated with homelessness contributes to mental and emotional problems, including the inability to focus and learn from regular classroom instruction (Fantuzzo, LeBoeuf, Chen, Rouse, & Culhane, 2012). Exclusion and ridicule by peers exacerbate mental and emotional problems, and can lead to behavior problems in school. Often school employees blame homeless children for displaying mental and emotional problems in their behavior without acknowledging, recognizing, or attempting to alleviate their pain (Barton, 2003).

In the previous chapter, an important part of teaching for unity discussed was ensuring that every student feels a sense of belongingness, connectedness, and identity with peers, the community, and the school. Teaching to restore builds upon and extends this aspect of teaching for unity to include advocacy for children experiencing personal trauma such as homelessness. Advocacy includes preparing and supporting homeless children in developing relationships with peers and helping other children to be inclusive in work and play. Advocacy includes privately interviewing homeless children to determine personal needs, including shelter, food, clothing, health, and hygiene. The teacher's interview can address feelings of personal safety, privacy, fear, and anxiety. The teacher can help children identify and access resources, including other professionals who can help, such as a social worker, school psychologist, and healthcare facilities. Homeless children often fall behind in schoolwork and need individualized instruction and coaching. Often homeless children are unable to remain after school for instructional support. Those living in shelters or other temporary government housing sometimes have access to tutors or homeschooling providers. Teachers can provide special instruction for those who assist children with homework assignments or remediation for gaps in knowledge or skills.

Beyond the classroom, schools have a commitment to being responsive to homeless children based on the McKinney-Vento Homeless Assistance Act 1987. Research revealed that in compliance with the McKinney-Vento Act, school districts have provided better services to homeless students, including professional development for teachers and other staff related to supporting homeless children and youth, transportation for students, school supplies, special education services, and relevant social services for families (Miller, 2011). Further, the McKinney-Vento Act requires that schools facilitate the enrollment of homeless children by waiving the usual document requirements and provide transportation to the home school when children move, if requested by parents. For more information on federal and state resources available for the homeless, go to https://nche.ed.gov.

## Children in Foster Care

Placement in foster care is a disruption of children's familial relationships caused by the loss of a stable caregiver due to death, incarceration, mental or physical incapacity, drug abuse, abandonment, neglect, child endangerment or abuse, or persistent homelessness. Placement in foster care removes children from situations that threaten their well-being and, for some children, mitigates stress and trauma. In 2016, over 400,000 children in the United States spent time in foster care. The average stay in foster care is 13.9 months; however, 4% of children remain in foster care for five or more years (U.S. Department of Health and Human Services, Children's Bureau, 2017). When possible, children reunite with their parents or other family members. Children remain in foster placement or are placed for adoption when parental rights are terminated.

Children experience severe trauma when separated from their parents or familiar caregivers. Instability in foster placement further exacerbates the negative impact of family separation. Many children will experience three or more foster care placements before entering kindergarten. Instability in the home environment and foster placement impact children's ability to develop relationships with individuals, as well as their growth and development (Pomeroy & Browning, 2010). This series of traumatic experiences has a particularly negative effect on a child's development of executive function, the ability to control personal attention and behavior. The impairment of executive function has a negative effect on learning and behavior management in school (Pears, Bruce, Fisher, Kim, & Yoerger, 2010).

Children who experience multiple foster care placements will often change schools several times while in elementary or high school. Moving from one foster placement to another and changing schools exacerbates the stress and trauma the child experiences when removed from family. Many children placed in foster care experience rejection and ridicule in school. The high level of stress and trauma caused by displacement from family, friends, and school can have a devastating effect on a child's academic, physical, psychological, and social well-being.

Usually, children placed in foster care have experienced major stress and trauma in their lives such as "early loss or lack of consistent caregivers; emotional, physical, or sexual abuse; domestic violence; various forms of neglect; natural disasters; medical and surgical procedures; and serious accidents" (Statman-Weil, 2015, pp. 72–73). The trauma children experience that results in removal from the home, in foster care, and in school has a negative impact on their mental and physical health. According to Bilaver, Jaudes, Koepke, and Goerge (1999):

> When compared with national standards and data, children in foster care register high levels of hearing and vision impairment, asthma, the toxic effects of lead, and tuberculosis; they also are more likely to suffer from problems associated with mental illness or developmental delays.
>
> *(p. 403)*

Wright and Ryan (2014) described the response to trauma as:

> The stress response system is hardwired to respond to trauma in one of three ways—fighting, freezing, or fleeing . . . That is, sometimes children demonstrate these responses through physical violence, refusal to move, or running out of the classroom. Other times these responses express themselves less obviously. For example, rather than physical violence, a child might fight teachers by refusing assistance, dismissing feedback, or breaking classroom rules . . . Freezing often results in children appearing inattentive or falling asleep in class . . . And, though physically present, children may be fleeing in their minds, distracted by traumatic flashbacks or consumed by fear. Consequently, many children who are traumatized may seem off-task, unsure of instructions, or disorganized in their thinking.
>
> *(p. 89)*

Children who display the behaviors described here often receive harsh discipline in school, including suspension, expulsion, and referral to law enforcement. However,

**TABLE 5.1** *Supplemental Performance Inventory*

Student _____
Grade/Subject _____
Teacher _____
Date _____

**Supplemental Performance Inventory**

**A. Academic Progress**
__Performs well on periodic assessments
__Completes assignments
__Participates in class activities
__Submits homework when due
__Submits homework late or incomplete
__Needs additional basic skills support in math, reading, oral communication, written communication
__Needs additional support for specific subject basic concepts
Suggestions (actions and materials):

**Physical Characteristics**
__Average energy level, alert, engaged
__Neat/clean physical appearance
__Low energy, slow moving, lacks stamina
__Sleeps in class
Suggestions (actions and materials):

**B. Psychological Development**
__Well-developed self-regulation and self-management
__Well-developed decision-making skills
__Well-developed analytical skills
__Self-confident, self-aware
Suggestions (actions and materials):

**C. Social Development**
__Well-developed social skills
__Needs support with social skills
__Positive relationships with peers
__Positive relationships with adults
__Follows class rules and protocols
__Emerging leadership skills
Suggestions (actions and materials):

children who have experienced trauma desperately need school to be a safe and supportive place where adults respond with understanding and compassion.

Children and youth in foster care need guidance in developing feelings of belongingness and connectedness in school. These children need to be encouraged to participate in activities where they can develop friendships with peers. Children need guidance in developing relationships with peers and some peers need guidance in developing relationships with those different from themselves. School support personnel, including school counselors, psychologists, and social workers, have special expertise in supporting students' social and psychological development. Periodic interviews and conversations with these trained school practitioners provide support and continuity in students' lives. Children need to feel comfortable initiating contact with these specialists, even if they move to another school. School support personnel can provide alternative emergency contact for students displaced from their families and those who experience instability in foster care placement. Further, school support personnel can interact with families in distress and caregivers for children displaced from their families, including foster parents.

An important predictor of students' performance in school is caregiver involvement. The interaction of school practitioners and foster caregivers is very limited. More than 65% of children and youth in foster care reported that their caregivers had never attended a teacher conference, visited their classroom, or volunteered at their school (Pears et al., 2010). Some foster parents feel constrained by limited knowledge of the child's prior school experience and short-term placements of less than one year. Teachers can support foster parents in feeling more connected with the child and the school by sending home a simple checklist report once or twice each month such as the *Supplemental Performance Inventory* (Table 5.1). Further, teachers can add suggestions to the checklist for resources that might be helpful to foster parents, including publications, videos, and websites.

Teachers can support children and youth placed in foster care through attention, recognition, and support in the classroom. Teachers give attention through careful observation of students' responses to instruction, class assignments, and during participation in small group work. Such observations help identify academic and social areas in need of coaching, guidance, or direct instruction. Recognition includes honest compliments and positive feedback on a personal action, quality, or accomplishment. Recognition is particularly important for encouraging self-regulation, building self-confidence, and supporting peer acceptance. Support in the classroom includes giving attention to social relationships when organizing small group work and team learning experiences. Each student placed in a small group or in pairs needs to feel accepted, included, and respected by peers when working collaboratively. Some students need direct instruction on how to work collaboratively in small groups and pairs. Other students need coaching or direct instruction on appropriate ways of interacting with peers perceived as different from themselves.

## Incarcerated Children

The United States has the highest rate of incarceration in the world. The United States has 5% of the world's population and 25% of the world's prison population.

The Pew Center reported that in 2008, 1 in 31 adults in the United States was incarcerated or on parole or probation. One in 45 adults was on probation and 1 in 100 was in prison or jail. This translates to 7.3 million adults in the United States under the control of the correction system. Among those under control of the correction system, 1 in 11 was African American, 1 in 27 was Hispanic, and 1 in 45 was White. In 2016, 2.2 million people in the United States were in jail or prison (Gramlich, 2018). This does not indicate that people of color commit more crimes or crimes that are more violent than do White people. This means that 1 in 14, or more than 5 million, children in the United States have a parent who lived with them go to jail or prison (Murphey & Cooper, 2015). The loss of a parent to incarceration deprives a child of parental attachment, guidance, and income. The absence of a parent puts the child at risk for toxic stress that contributes to difficulties in school, school dropout, poor healthcare, and placement in foster care. The adverse effects of losing a parent places the child at risk for contact with law enforcement and ultimately juvenile detention.

Children who have experienced trauma and toxic stress enter school having developed coping skills that work in their home and community environment, but not in school. It is unusual for schools to have a planned curriculum for socializing children into the practices, routines, and rules of school. However, school practitioners punish children for aggressive, impulsive, out-of-control behavior, emotional and social difficulties, and difficulties learning, focusing attention, and following directions. These behaviors are beyond the child's control without coaching, guidance, and direct instruction from adults. Yet according to Heitzeg (2014):

> Rather than creating an atmosphere of learning, engagement, and opportunity, current educational practices have increasingly blurred the distinction between school and jail. The school to prison pipeline refers to this growing pattern of tracking students out of educational institutions, primarily via "zero tolerance" policies, and tracking them directly and/or indirectly into the juvenile and adult criminal justice systems.
>
> *(p. 12)*

This process of tracking children into the juvenile and adult criminal justice systems begins in preschool, continues through high school, and includes children with medically diagnosed disabilities.

The U.S. Department of Education, Office of Civil Rights (2014a) reported that in 2011–2012, the total enrollment in elementary and secondary schools was 49 million students. During the 2011–2012 school year, 3.5 million students were suspended in school, 3.5 million were suspended out of school, and 130,000 students were expelled. Additionally, 260,000 students received referrals to law enforcement and 92,000 students experienced school-related arrests. African American students had the highest rate of suspension and expulsion, which was three times greater than for White students. African American students represented 16% of school enrollment, 27% of referrals to law enforcement, and 31% of school-related arrests.

The U.S. Department of Education, Office of Civil Rights (2014b) responded to the treatment and impact of disciplinary practices in these data with an advice and guidance letter dated January 8, 2014. This letter cautioned school officials about discipline policies with a *different treatment* for particular groups of students and those that have a *disparate impact* for particular groups of students. Examples for different treatment and disparate impact were included in the letter. The following is an example of different treatment:

> A complainant alleges that her eighth-grade son, who is African-American, was referred to the office at his school and received a one-day in-school suspension for "use of profane or vulgar language"—a Level 1 offense— during a class period. The disciplinary sanction imposed was within the permissible range for Level 1 offenses. The student has had no previous discipline incidents. A White student at the same school and with a similar disciplinary history also committed a Level 1 offense: "inappropriate display of affection" while on the school bus. While the parent of the White student was called, the student received no additional disciplinary sanction.
>
> *(p. 15)*

The different treatment in this example also has a disparate impact in that the African American student does not have access to classroom instruction, while the White student benefits from classroom instruction and interaction with peers.

The U.S. Department of Education, Office of Civil Rights (2014b) presented three questions to determine if a school or district policy or practices result in illegal acts of racial discrimination (disparate impact) or intentional discrimination (different treatment):

1. Has the discipline policy resulted in an adverse impact on students of a particular race as compared with students of other races?
2. Is the discipline policy necessary to meet an important educational goal?
3. Are there comparably effective alternative policies or practices that would meet the school's stated educational goal with less of a burden or adverse impact on the disproportionately affected racial group, or is the school's proffered justification a pretext for discrimination?

These are questions used to investigate claims submitted to the U.S. Department of Education by parents or legal guardians concerning discriminatory disciplinary policies and practices in schools, districts, and classrooms.

Those most likely to receive harsh discipline are students who have experienced trauma or toxic stress in their lives within and/or outside of school. Toxic stress is a condition resulting from frequent and/or prolonged adversity that can affect a child's brain structure and chemistry. Trauma and toxic stress inhibit the development of metacognitive processes of executive function (self-regulation) that enable planning, controlling, and organizing thoughts, emotions, and behaviors (Cutuli & Herbers, 2014). Harsh discipline does not enable the metacognitive processes of executive function that support self-regulation. Instead, harsh punishment increases the stress and trauma that thwart students' ability to focus attention and learn to control behaviors and emotions. Students need guidance, coaching, and direct instruction to support learning metacognitive processes that support self-regulation. Further, without the guidance of trusted adults, these students are unlikely to develop self-regulation.

The cumulative effects of multiple suspensions and expulsions can be devastating for children who have experienced trauma and toxic stress. Many youngsters withdraw and ultimately drop out of school. Others become increasingly frustrated, agitated, and confused. The ability to control their behavior and emotions further deteriorates. Learning difficulties escalate as stress increases. If these children remain in school, the likelihood increases for referral to law enforcement and school-related arrests for minor infractions of school rules and non-criminal and nonviolent antisocial behavior. Examples of nonviolent antisocial behaviors include using inappropriate language, insubordination, truancy, talking back to a teacher, tardiness, acting out or disrupting class, and tantrums. School practitioners will have completed the cycle of disruption in the lives of the most vulnerable children by placing them in the juvenile justice system. Children are less likely to return to normalcy in life after incarceration.

School-related arrests initiate direct contact with the juvenile justice system. According to a report from the U.S. Department of Justice, Office of Juvenile Justice and Delinquency Prevention (2018), in 2016, law enforcement agencies in the United States arrested more than 856,000 youth under 18 years of age. This was down from the more than 1 million youth arrested in 2015, and in six states law enforcement arrested more than 5% of the total population of children. In 2015, about 48,000 youngsters were in residential placement on an average night. Black children had the highest residential placement. The courts placed about 1,000 children in adult prisons. Children having experienced trauma and toxic stress, and those with special needs, are particularly vulnerable to victimization in juvenile detention and adult prisons.

The school is a primary generative source for youth involvement with the juvenile justice system, yet when released from detention the expectation is that these youngsters will return to school and succeed. The assumption is that the experience of detention alone taught these youngsters the social skills and self-regulation they need to succeed in school and in life. Instead, these youngsters return to school with more reproachable behaviors and perceptions learned from peers in the juvenile detention system, as well as a negative personal identity, that contribute to further alienation from peers and adults in school. Administrators and teachers are not usually prepared to support the re-entry of youngsters who have been court-involved. Often these youngsters face resistance from school administrators who perceive them as difficult to manage. Some states prohibit court-involved youth from re-entering public schools and mandate alternative school attendance (Thomas, 2014).

Many youngsters who experience repeated harsh school discipline and those involved with the courts have underdeveloped skills related to executive function. Other students have special needs that have caused developmental delays in executive function. Punishment is not effective for teaching or learning these skills. Cutuli and Herbers (2014) define executive function as "the metacognitive processes that help plan, control, and organize thoughts, feelings and behaviors toward some goal" (p. 119). These authors define self-regulation as "the child or adolescent's level of executive functioning and ability to control his or her emotions and behavior" (p. 119). Self-regulation is essential for success in school and in life. The component skills for self-regulation described by Zimmerman (2002) include:

> (a) setting specific proximal *goals* for oneself, (b) adopting powerful *strategies* for attaining the goals, (c) *monitoring* one's performance selectively for signs of progress, (d) *restructuring* one's physical and social context to make it compatible with one's goals, (e) managing one's time *use* efficiently, (f) *self-evaluating* one's methods, (g) *attributing* causation to results, and (h) *adapting* future methods.
>
> *(p. 66)*

Supporting students in developing self-regulation requires embedding in their everyday learning experiences opportunities for internalizing specific skills and values (Table 5.2). Traditional practices of teaching students to follow a set of

**TABLE 5.2** Self-regulation skills and values

| *Values* | *Skills* |
| --- | --- |
| Adaptability | Focus attention |
| Cooperation | Forethought (anticipation, investigation) |
| Helpfulness | Goal-setting |
| Honesty | Task analysis |
| Integrity | Strategic planning |
| Perseverance | Task completion |
| Personal initiative | Reflection |
| Responsibility | Causal attribution |
| Respectfulness | |
| Self-control | |
| Trustworthiness | |

**TABLE 5.3** *Weekly Self-Management Plan*

Name: _____

Grade/Subject:_____

Teacher:_____

Date:_____

**Weekly Self-Management Plan***

1. Accomplishments made this week
    a. Assignments


    b. Personal development (attributes, values, approaches, practices)


2. Challenges this week


3. Plans for next week
    a. Assignments


    b. Personal development (attributes, values, approaches, practices)


4. Challenges anticipated for next week

    a. Strategies for addressing anticipated challenges

5. My personal assets

6. Help needed

---

* **Submit to teacher every Friday.**

classroom rules help keep order in the classroom but are insufficient or unreliable for supporting the basic tenets of self-regulation. However, socializing students into specific procedures and routines that reinforce clearly identified skills and values help maintain order in the classroom and support the development of self-regulation. Direct instruction strategies that support self-regulation related to specific skills and values include demonstration, modeling, guided practice, coaching, cueing, assessment and feedback. Indirect instruction engages students in independent inquiry and problem-solving. For example, students can be encouraged to read multiple pieces of literature where analyzing and comparing characters results in a deep understanding of the target skills and values. The *Weekly Self-Management Plan* (Table 5.3) is appropriate for use with students who need consistent and structured monitoring, support, and feedback to develop self-regulation. This tool incorporates skills that support the development of self-regulation and several essential values, including adaptability, perseverance, personal initiative, and responsibility. It is important for the teacher to provide immediate feedback that acknowledges persistence and progress in developing the skills and values that support self-regulation.

## Immigrant Children

The United States has been the top destination of choice for international immigrants for over five decades. In 2017, one-fifth of the world's migrants lived in the United States (Zong, Batalova, & Hallock, 2018). About 14% (45 million) of all residents of the United States are foreign-born (Pew Research Center, 2015). The majority of recent immigrants, about 80%, arrive from Latin America, Asia, Africa, Oceania, and the Caribbean. These demographic changes in the population place new demands on classroom teachers for new knowledge and teaching practices that support the adjustment, growth, and development of children from immigrant families. Teaching students from immigrant families requires that teachers understand the experiential backgrounds of the children, their developmental needs, and that teachers develop the ability to communicate with immigrant children and families.

Children from immigrant families live in different home environments and have different background experiences. Researchers describe different types of immigrant families that include mixed parents where one parent is an immigrant, foreign-born children with two immigrant parents, and U.S.-born children with two immigrant parents (Borjas, 2011). Other descriptions of immigrant families include transnational, refugee, and mixed-status families (Sanchez, 2014). Twenty-five percent of children under the age of 18 have at least one parent who is an immigrant. Among children from immigrant families, 81% have parents who speak English and another language at home, and 5% of immigrant families do not have a parent or caregiver who speaks English. There is wide variation of family income among immigrants based on education and race.

About 24% of immigrant children come from low-income families (Crosnoe & Lopez Turley, 2011). Nearly half of immigrant children live in households that receive some form of public assistance (Borjas, 2011). The educational levels of parents in immigrant families varies widely. However, in 2016, approximately 30% of all foreign-born adults over the age of 25 living in the United States had earned at least a bachelor's degree. This was slightly lower than for U.S.-born adults in the same age group, with 32% of adults with at least a bachelor's degree (Zong et al., 2018). About 26% of immigrant families do not include a parent with a high school diploma (Crosnoe & Lopez Turley, 2011). However, a higher percentage of Asian and African immigrant families tend to have better-educated parents than others, including those with U.S.-born parents.

Children from immigrant families come to school with different levels of preparation and readiness. The U.S. Department of Homeland Security (2018) reported that in 2017, 365,682 H-1B specialty occupation visas were issued. This is a temporary visa issued for six years to non-citizens with specialty skills not readily available in the United States. Parents holding H-1B visas are well-educated, speak English, and usually provide many educational opportunities for their children. Children from these families come to school ready to learn. Children from refugee families have fled war, violence, famine, and other politically and socially disruptive, and life-threatening, situations. Some children from refugee families suffer post-traumatic stress disorder and developmental delays resulting from their experiences enduring and escaping tumultuous conditions. Children with one or more undocumented family members live in fear of having their families disrupted by deportation. Other children immigrating to the United States experience trauma in separating from family, friends, and the familiar environment of their country of origin, and in adjusting to a new environment. In the process of resettlement, some children experience detention similar to incarceration. Many of these experiences have a long-term negative impact on children's growth and development academically, psychologically, and socially.

In general, students from immigrant families perform academically as well or better than their U.S.-born peers (Crosnoe & Lopez Turley, 2011). Data from the National Assessment of Educational Progress (NAEP, 2015) revealed that in the United States, not a single subgroup has 50% or more of students performing at the level of proficient or above in reading or mathematics at twelfth grade. This means that more than 50% of students in all subgroups perform below grade level expectations in reading and mathematics at twelfth grade. However, Asian students consistently outperform their peers, including White students, in reading and mathematics in twelfth grade on the NAEP standardized assessment. Children from Southeast Asia do not tend to perform as well as other Asian students. Children from immigrant families originating in Latin America do not perform as well as their Asian or U.S.-born White peers. The immigrant paradox is the fact that students from Asia, Africa, and the Caribbean tend to outperform their U.S.-born peers. A partial explanation for the paradox is that children in families from specific immigrant groups more often than their U.S.-born peers have parents with a bachelor's degree or higher. Another explanation given for this paradox is that teachers favor students from more educated family backgrounds (Crosnoe & Lopez Turley, 2011).

Based on academic performance, children in families originating from countries in Asia, Africa, and the Caribbean may not need as much academic support as many of their peers. However, these children may have experienced trauma and toxic stress due to relocation and separation from extended family members, friends, and familiar cultural practices in their home countries. Additionally, immigrant children may experience isolation and exclusion by their U.S.-born peers. One explanation for this response from U.S.-born students is that many friendship groups formed outside of school or formed within school prior to the arrival of their immigrant peers. Further, some children are from refugee families fleeing societal upheaval, political dissolution, war, and violence. These children are likely to have experienced trauma and toxic stress requiring support similar to that discussed earlier in this chapter for U.S.-born children with related experiences and psychological responses. Children from immigrant families, especially those who have experienced trauma and toxic stress, require support for learning U.S. cultural norms and practices, and building relationships with other children, including their U.S.-born peers. Monitoring immigrant students' adjustment to the classroom culture is important. Using the *Student Observation Inventory* (Table 5.5) might be helpful.

The number of children classified as English learners living in the United States exceeds 5 million. This is more than 10% of all students enrolled in elementary and secondary schools in the United States. The majority of children who are English learners were born in the United States. Most preservice teacher preparation programs provide training in using a variety of approaches for supporting children in developing English language proficiency. School districts offer professional development for teachers in using the specific approach implemented locally. School districts subscribe to one of three models and related programs for developing children's competence in English. The three models for developing English language competence include dual language, transitional bilingual education, and English only. Dual language is an additive approach that maintains the native language while learning a new language. Transitional bilingual education provides initial support for the native language while learning English as a second language, but over time decreases support for the native language in favor of emphasis on developing proficiency in English. English only emphasizes proficiency and literacy in English. Examples of English only approaches include sheltered English instruction, English as a second language, and structured English immersion (Sugarman, 2018). The expectation in each model is that English learners develop competence in conversational English and academic language. Competence in academic language supports students in learning academic subjects.

## Application to Practice

Many children have a wide variety of experiences within and outside of school that contribute to trauma and toxic stress. Examples of such experiences include abuse, abandonment, neglect, family separation, and immigration. This chapter includes a series of tools that can be used to assess students' needs, provide support for growth and development, and monitor students' progress. The following discussion provides guidance for the application of these tools to practice.

The first step in applying information from this chapter and preparing for teaching students at any grade level, in any subject area or context, is conducting at least a general pre-assessment of students' experience and development academically, psychologically, and socially. Using appropriate instruments, such as the *Student Development Inventory* (Table 5.4) and the *Student Observation Inventory* (Table 5.5) included in this chapter, makes initial pre-assessment data collection and analysis efficient and productive. Parents complete the *Student Development Inventory* for younger children. Parents and students each complete the *Student Development Inventory* at the middle and secondary school levels. The *Student Development Inventory* should be submitted well in advance of the first day of school. Middle and secondary parents and students complete the *Student Development Inventory* for corroboration of information, and to initiate the practice of self-assessment and personal reflection for students. Self-assessment and personal reflection are essential aspects in the development of executive function, especially self-regulation. Further, data from these inventories can be useful for collaborating with medical and mental healthcare professionals, as discussed in Chapter 6.

Ideally, the *Student Observation Inventory* (Table 5.5) is conducted during the first two weeks of school. The *Student Observation Inventory* provides useful information about every student; however, this inventory can be used selectively in responding only to students with areas of concern identified in the *Student Development Inventory* (Table 5.4) completed by parents and students. The *Student Observation Inventory* further corroborates data from the *Student Development Inventory*. The categories are the same in each inventory, but the elements vary to provide complementary perspectives. For example, students expressing dissatisfaction with schoolwork to family and friends at home helps explain academic performance in school and informs teaching practices. If the *Student Development Inventory* indicates that the student has been recommended for repeating a grade for a second year or failed one or more middle or high school subjects and struggled with basic skills, this helps explain why the student does not complete and return homework when it is due. The information from the *Student Development Inventory* and the *Student Observation Inventory* indicate the need for additional learning experiences to support the development of basic skills.

**TABLE 5.4** *Student Development Inventory*

Student: _____

Parent: _____

Date: _____

**Student Development Inventory**
Please check any statements below that apply to you during the previous school year.

**A. Academic**
___ Reads for pleasure regularly.
___Traveled to a country outside the United States in the past 18 months.
___ Enjoyed the challenge of learning new skills and subject matter.
___ Completed and submitted homework when due.
___ Complained about homework.
___ Struggled with basic skills in reading or mathematics.
___ Recommended for repeating the same grade (1st, 2nd, 3rd, 4th, 5th, 6th, 7th, 8th).
___ Failed one or more subjects or courses (English, math, history, science, etc.).
___ Resisted attending school.
___ Changed schools one or more times during the school year.
___ Speaks English as a second language.
**B. Physical**
___ Eats regularly scheduled and balanced meals.
___ Access to a safe place to play and exercise outside of school (yard, playground, park, etc.).
___ Regular schedule of sleep, exercise, and recreation.
___ Missed three or more days of school due to illness.
**C. Psychological**
___ Lived at home with parents and siblings.
___ Lost someone or something personally important (family member, friend, pet, etc.).
___ Immigrated to the United States in the past three years.
___ Experienced personal trauma (illness, accident, violence, natural disaster, etc.).
___ Felt sad, disappointed, preoccupied, or distracted for more than a few days.
___ Felt angry, disrespected, or violated by an incident, relationship, or situation.
___ Felt unsafe at home, school, or other place of required attendance.
___ Felt uncomfortable talking with adults (parents, teachers, counselors, administrators, etc.).
___ Felt alone or isolated.
___ Felt happy with the present and hopeful for the future.
___ Spent more than two hours daily on the Internet or playing video games.
___ Engaged in activities that are age-inappropriate or illegal (smoking, alcohol, drugs, sex, etc.).
**D. Social**
___ Enjoyed time with family.
___ Enjoyed attending school with friends.
___ Enjoyed time outside of school with friends.
___ Experienced name-calling and humiliation from peers.
___ Experienced bullying from one or more peers, in person or online.
___ Actions and suggestions from teachers and administrators did not resolve concerns.
___ Parent conferences with teachers and administrators did not resolve concerns.

**TABLE 5.5** *Student Observation Inventory*

---

Student: _____

Grade/Subject: _____

Teacher: _____

Date: _____

**Student Observation Inventory**

Please check any of the statements below that apply to this student.

**A. Academic Engagement**

__ Academically competent and confident.

__ Shows initiative, creativity, and originality.

__ Completes and submits assignments when due.

__ Stays focused and on task.

__ Works well individually.

__ Works well in small groups.

__ Takes leadership role spontaneously.

**B. Physical Characteristics**

__ Average energy level, alert, engaged.

__ Low energy, slow-moving, lacks stamina.

__ Sleeps in class.

__ Poor physical coordination.

__ Poor posture.

__ Taller/shorter than average for age/grade level.

__ Attention-getting or distracting physical attributes.

__ Neat/clean physical appearance.

**C. Psychological Disposition**

__ Confident/self-regulation.

__ Excessively gregarious.

__ Shy and withdrawn.

__ Impulsive/easily distracted.

__ Melancholy/sad, preoccupied.

__ Feels persecuted by peers and the world.

**D. Social Interaction/Relationships**

__ Personable, outgoing, friendly.

__ Well-developed social skills.

__ Favored by peers.

__ Isolated/rejected by peers.

__ Engaged in disruptive/disrespectful behavior.

---

The second step in applying information from this chapter is developing an efficient structured approach for supporting, monitoring, and providing feedback for students who have experienced trauma and toxic stress that impacted the metacognitive processes of executive function (self-regulation) that enable planning, controlling, and organizing thoughts, emotions, and behaviors. The complexity of managing a classroom where a high percentage of students have experienced stress and trauma can be overwhelming for new teachers. The use of appropriate instruments such as the *Weekly Self-Management Plan* (Table 5.3) and the *Supplemental Performance Inventory* (Table 5.1) reduce the complexity for meeting individual needs in a highly diverse group of students. The *Weekly Self-Management Plan* supports students in developing executive function through an iterative and repetitive procedure of documentation of accomplishments, challenges, and assets that engages the cognitive processes of reflection, planning, analysis, and anticipation. Additionally, students choose a value or skill from the list provided to support personal development (Table 5.2). This iterative and repetitive procedure and cognitive process supports the development of self-regulation when used weekly with students whose executive function has been compromised. Younger children will need support and coaching to complete this procedure and cognitive process. Beginning in third grade through high school, students should be able to work independently in completing this procedure. The teacher provides brief feedback that acknowledges the effort with a rating (inadequate, minimal, adequate, or advanced) or guidance (clarify, edit, elaborate, or revise). The *Supplemental Performance Inventory* is a tool for student self-assessment and for feedback to parents on a student's academic, social, and psychological development.

The third step in applying information from this chapter is incorporating into the curriculum and learning experiences the procedures, processes, and values that support and strengthen executive function. The curriculum content incorporates and highlights the values associated with the development of executive function (Table 5.2). For example, the study of leading historical personalities emphasizes these values. These values are explicit in the literature for English language arts, especially in biographies. Learning experiences incorporate the skills associated with executive function (Table 5.2). An example of a specific technique used to focus students' attention is advance organizers. Steele (2008) pointed out that "advance organizers are beneficial for students that have difficulty with attention, auditory processing, and listening skills" (p. 198). Graphic organizers and outlines are examples of advance organizers. Steele (2008) provides a table that summarizes other teaching modifications for middle school social studies designed for students experiencing learning difficulties. Roscoe and Orr (2010) indicate that advance organizers for teaching science include learning objectives, main idea, and introducing lessons with science activities that focus attention on the science concept under consideration.

Finally, teaching is a highly complex process that requires the application of highly specialized knowledge of learners, learning, subject matter, and pedagogy. Ensuring that students with challenging life conditions and experiences have their specific developmental needs met, and that all students have meaningful and productive learning experiences that result in meeting grade level and subject area expectations, is a tremendous cognitive load for classroom teachers. The instruments described in the three steps in the application to practice

**TABLE 5.6** *Teaching Practices Inventory*

---

Teacher: _____
Grade/Subject: _____
Date: _____

**Teaching Practices Inventory**

**Academic Engagement**
___ Academic content and skills embedded in meaningful learning experiences link to appropriate state and national standards.
___ Students engage in inquiry-based, problem-based, project-based, or multidimensional experiences that provide opportunities for learning basic skills, discipline-specific practices, and application to real life.
___ Students have opportunities to work individually and collaboratively.
___ Students have several options for demonstrating progress in meeting expectations for competencies and standards.
___ Students are provided appropriate accommodation for meeting grade level and subject matter expectations and standards, including prerequisite knowledge and skills.
___ Learning experiences and assignments address the needs of students living with the effects of stress, trauma, or displacement.

**Social Interaction**
___ Social skills and core values embedded in learning experiences support students' developmental needs.
___ Students have opportunities to interact and build relationships with peers different from themselves.
___ Social situations with supportive peers are arranged for students who are shy, withdrawn, or experience exclusion or isolation.

**Psychological Disposition**
___ Students receive support for developing self-confidence and self-regulation.
___ Students receive support for developing perspectives of hopefulness and optimism.
___ Students receive encouragement and praise when appropriate.
___ Students experiencing the effects of trauma and displacement receive attention and support.

**Physical Characteristics**
___ Students with special physical challenges and needs receive appropriate accommodation.
___ Seating is appropriate for students' physical height and size.
___ Correct posture and carriage are encouraged.
___ Breaks and exercise accommodate students' physical needs.

---

approach help ameliorate teachers' cognitive load. The final instrument in the series, the *Teaching Practices Inventory* (Table 5.6), supports teachers in assessing the completeness of their own practice in the key developmental areas for students. The content in this final instrument links to that of the other instruments in the series. The *Teaching Practices Inventory* assists teachers in reviewing the consistency and continuity in their own instructional planning and enables strategic improvement in teaching practices.

## Chapter Summary

This chapter addresses teaching to restore the academic, psychological, and social well-being of children and youth who experience trauma in their lives, including alienation, isolation, rejection, abandonment, displacement, neglect, and victimization. The discussion addresses approaches to classroom support for students living with peer rejection, distracted parents, in poverty, homeless, in extended families, in foster care, group homes, incarcerated, and those who are immigrants, especially refugees. Teaching to restore addresses the needs of children who have experienced trauma and toxic stress that compromises or threatens the full development of metacognitive processes of executive function (self-regulation) that enable planning, controlling, and organizing thoughts, emotions, and behaviors.

Children and youth experience trauma and toxic stress within and outside of school. Children who face challenges outside of school are at risk for experiencing challenges in school related to their academic performance, social relationships, and psychological development. Many children who have experienced trauma and toxic stress have not learned to manage their own behavior and relationships with peers because they have not had the adult guidance and support necessary for developing social skills and self-regulation. School practitioners often respond to these children's developmental needs with harsh punishment rather than guidance and support. Harsh punishment will not teach children and youth the social skills and self-regulation they need to succeed in school and in life. Thus, these children are often retained in the same grade for a second year in elementary school, struggle with basic skills in reading and mathematics, fail subjects in high school, drop out of high school, have early encounters with law enforcement, and some will be incarcerated as adults.

Teaching social skills and self-regulation requires careful observation, data collection, planning, instruction, coaching, monitoring, and assessment. The use of appropriate instruments increases time efficiency and productivity in data collection, monitoring, and assessment. Supporting students in developing self-regulation requires embedding in their everyday learning experiences opportunities for internalizing specific skills and values. Target values that support social skills and self-regulation are central to the curriculum, and are found in characters in children and adolescent literature and in historical biographies. Skills for self-regulation are the academic procedures and processes that form the core of learning experiences and assignments. Teaching in this way diminishes the need for harsh punishment and provides children and youth with the guidance and support necessary for developing the social skills and academic competency essential for success in school and in life.

In the application to practice discussion, the developmental needs of children and youth are identified and incorporated into the curriculum and instructional practices through a series of data collection instruments. The elements in each of the instruments support the growth and development of children academically, psychologically, and socially. Special attention is focused on the development of executive function, self-regulation that enables the child to control personal attention and behavior. Self-regulation increases the probability for success in school and in life.

## References

Barton, A. C. (2003). Kobe's story: Doing science as contested terrain. *Qualitative Studies in Education*, 16(4), 533–552.

Bilaver, L. A., Jaudes, P. K., Koepke, D., & Goerge, R. M. (1999). The health of children in foster care. *Social Service Review*, 73(3), 401–417.

Borjas, G. J. (2011). Poverty and program participation among immigrant children. *The Future of Children*, 21(1), 247–266.

Crosnoe, R. & Lopez Turley, R. N. (2011). K-12 educational outcomes of immigrant youth. *The Future of Children*, 21(1), 129–152.

Cutuli, J. J. & Herbers, J. E. (2014). Promoting resilience for children who experience family homelessness: Opportunities to encourage developmental competence. *Cityscape*, 16(1), 113–140.

Duger, A. (2015). Focusing on prevention: The social and economic rights of children vulnerable to sex trafficking. *Health and Human Rights*, 17(1), 114–123.

Fantuzzo, J. W., LeBoeuf, W. A., Chen, C., Rouse, H. L., & Culhane, D. P. (2012). The unique and combined effects of homelessness and school mobility on the educational outcomes of young children. *Educational Researcher*, 41(9), 393–402.

Gramlich, J. (2018). *America's incarceration rate is at a two-decade low*. Washington, DC: Pew Research Center.

Heitzeg, N. A. (2014). Criminalizing education: Zero tolerance policies, police in the hallways, and the school to prison pipeline. *Counterpoints*, 453, 11–36.

MacGillivray, L., Ardell, A. L., & Curwen, M. S. (2010). Supporting the literacy development of children living in homeless shelters. *The Reading Teacher*, 63(5), 384–392.

McDowell, R., Dunklin, R., Schmall, E., & Pritchard, J. (2017, May 2). *Hidden horror of school sex assaults revealed by AP*. Retrieved from https://apnews.com/1b74feef88df44 75b377dcdd6406ebb7.

Miller, P. M. (2011). A critical analysis of the research on student homelessness. *Educational Researcher*, 81(3), 308–337.

Mitchell, M. W. (2010). Child sexual abuse: A school leadership issue. *The Clearing House*, 83(3), 101–104.

Murphey, D. & Cooper, P. M. (2015). *Parents behind bars: What happens to their children?* Bethesda, MD: Child Trends.

Murphy, J. F. & Tobin, K. J. (2011). Homelessness comes to school: How homeless children and youth can succeed. *The Phi Delta Kappan*, 93(3), 32–37.

National Center for Educational Statistics (NAEP) (2015). *National Assessment of Educational Progress*. Washington, DC: Institute of Education Sciences, U.S. Department of Education.

National Center for Education Statistics (2017). *Indicators of school crime and safety: Indicator 11: Bullying at school and cyberbullying anywhere*. Washington, DC: Institute for Education Sciences, U.S. Department of Education.

Pears, K. C., Bruce, J., Fisher, P. A., Kim, H. K., & Yoerger, K. (2010). Early elementary school adjustment of maltreated children in foster care: The roles of inhibitory control and caregiver involvement. *Child Development*, 1(5), 1550–1564.

Pew Research Center (2015, September 28). *Modern Immigration wave brings 59 million to U.S., driving population growth and change through 2065*. Washington, DC: Author.

Pomeroy, E. C. & Browning, P. (2010). Youths in crisis. *Social Work*, 55(3), 197–201.

Roscoe, K. & Orr, K. (2010). Frontloading classroom management: How to plan for the first class. *The Science Teacher*, 77(5), 43–48.

Sanchez, P. (2014). Research policy: Dignifying every day policies and practice that impact immigrant students. *Language Arts*, 91(5), 363–371.

Shakeshaft, C. (2004). *Educator sexual misconduct: A synthesis of existing literature*. Washington, DC: U.S. Department of Education, Office of the Under Secretary.

Shakeshaft, C. (2013). Know the warning signs of educator sexual misconduct. *The Phi Delta Kappan*, 94(5), 8–13.

Statman-Weil, K. (2015). Preschool through grade 3: Creating trauma-sensitive classrooms. *YC Young Children*, 70(2), 72–79.

Steele, M. M. (2008). Teaching social studies to middle school students with learning problems. *The Clearing House*, 81(5), 197–200.

Sugarman, J. (2018). *A matter of design: English learner program models in K-12 education*. Washington, DC: Migration Policy Institute, National Center on Immigrant Integration Policy. Retrieved from www.migrationpolicy.org/integration.

Thomas, A. B. (2014). Youth in transition and school reentry: Process, problems, and preparation. *Counterpoints*, 453, 248–259.

U.S. Department of Education, Office of Civil Rights (2014a). *Civil rights data collection. Data snapshot: School discipline*. Washington, DC: Author.

U.S. Department of Education, Office of Civil Rights (2014b). *Notice of language assistance: Dear colleague letter on the nondiscriminatory administration of school discipline*. Washington, DC: Author.

U.S. Department of Health and Human Services, Children's Bureau (2017). *Child welfare information gateway: Foster care statistics 2016*. Washington, DC: Author.

U.S. Department of Homeland Security (2018, April 9). *Characteristics of H-1B specialty occupation workers*. Washington, DC: Author.

U.S. Department of Justice, Office of Juvenile Justice and Delinquency Prevention (2018). *Juvenile justice statistics: National report series bulletin*. Washington, DC: Author.

Walter, J. S. (2018). Teacher license revocation and surrender in North Carolina due to sexual misconduct. *Journal of Music Teacher Education*, 1–15.

Wildeman, C. (2014). Parental incarceration, child homelessness, and the invisible consequences of mass incarceration. *The Annals of the American Academy of Political and Social Science*, 651, 74–96.

Wright, T. & Ryan, S. K. (2014). Toddlers through primary grades: Too scared to learn: Teaching young children who have experienced trauma. *YC Young Children*, 69(5), 88–93.

Zimmerman, B. J. (2002). Becoming a self-regulated learner: An overview. *Theory into Practice*, 41(2), 64–70.

Zong, J., Batalova, J., & Hallock, J. (2018, February 8). *Frequently requested statistics on immigrants and immigration in the United States*. Washington, DC: Migration Policy Institute. Retrieved from www.migrationpolicy.org.

# 6

# COLLABORATING WITH OTHER PROFESSIONALS

## Supporting Children and Youth with Acute Emotional, Mental, and Social Conditions

*Curtis W. Branch*

CLINICAL PSYCHOLOGIST, PRIVATE PRACTICE, HACKENSACK, NEW JERSEY

## Focus Questions

1. How do teachers determine when a child needs to be evaluated by a medical or mental health professional?
2. What data kept by teachers are useful to medical and mental health professionals in evaluating a child, making a diagnosis, and developing an intervention?
3. What types of instructional practices best support children with emotional, mental, or social conditions?

## Introduction

The presence of children with special emotional needs in the classroom often presents significant challenges for teachers. Many of those challenges can be overcome by the introduction of new data that will assist teachers in developing pedagogical strategies that are rooted in clinical and research findings about conditions which often cause children to be disconnected from learning and social environments. This chapter is designed to provide teachers with an overview of three common conditions that have been the subject of much recent discussion—depression, post-traumatic stress disorder, and gang affiliation. Each of these conditions has the potential for causing children to be disconnected from others, including themselves. The chapter is a mixture of new clinical data about the specific conditions and suggestions for teachers to consider when planning learning experiences for students.

Clinical data presented in this chapter are drawn from research sources in psychology and psychiatry. Some of it may appear to be only tangentially related to the task of teaching. That is not the case. It is essential that teachers understand the complexity and depth of cognitive and behavioral symptoms students experience in devising effective strategies for ameliorating symptoms that challenge student learning. The chapter is divided into three areas, with a closing section on implications for teachers. Finally, there are questions that teachers can use to guide application of the information presented throughout the chapter.

## Post-Traumatic Stress Disorder

Post-traumatic stress disorder (PTSD) is a clinical disorder that has a long past but a short history. Over the past 25 years, the frequency with which American children have experienced traumatic events has been increasingly documented. Causes of trauma that have been thoroughly researched and reported include child abuse, domestic and community violence, natural disasters, war, and refugee conditions. It is estimated that approximately 10% of children exposed to traumatic events will develop full-blown post-traumatic stress disorder. PTSD in children and adolescents looks very different from the disorder in adults. A widely held view of PTSD is that it is a disorder that occurs exclusively among individuals who have experienced the trauma of military combat duty. That is not true. There is PTSD that is rooted in combat, but there is also non-combat PTSD, which has been reported in children, adolescents, and adults. The current discussion is limited to non-combat PTSD as it occurs in children and adolescents. Moreover, there is evidence that many of the myths surrounding the disorder are frequently accepted as being true, and therefore become the basis of unfounded assumptions about the disorder and its impact on learning and social behavior. Specifically, there is a recent trend toward believing that all exposure to trauma will lead to the development of PTSD. In this chapter, research data regarding the individual symptoms of PTSD (i.e. exposure to violence) and their relevance to learning difficulties in the classroom will be examined. A detailed schema for distinguishing symptoms and signs for a fully developed and specifically diagnosed PTSD disorder will be presented. The label or designation of PTSD should be used only after the diagnosis has been established by a licensed mental health professional. Applying the label by persons other than a mental health professional constitutes unethical and in some cases illegal behavior, which could result in legal penalties and sanctions! Before making a diagnosis of PTSD, the mental health clinician should examine the child and complete a detailed psychosocial history. Four critical conditions must be met before the diagnosis of PTSD can be made: exposure to a traumatic event, re-experiencing the trauma, avoidance and numbing, and hyperarousal.

### *Exposure to a Traumatic Event*

In a diagnosis of PTSD, the child must have been exposed to an extreme traumatic stressor that consisted of either direct personal experience or witnessing an event involving the threat of death, serious injury, or other threat to one's personal integrity or learning about unexpected or violent death, serious harm, or threat of death or injury experienced by one's family member or close associate (peer, teacher, babysitter) (Sadock, Sadock, & Ruiz, 2009). This criterion is sometimes difficult to establish because of selective reporting by the child victim. However, there is the possibility that children with very active imaginations may create in their mind events that never really happened. Then there is the possibility that a child may interpret an event as being traumatic but others who are aware of the event may assess it very differently. It is the child's reality that eventually decides what is traumatic and what is not. A mental health professional who is skilled at interviewing children can prove priceless in determining if a child had an experience that meets the clinical standard for being considered traumatic.

## Re-Experiencing

In re-experiencing, the traumatic event is experienced by the child multiple times after it occurs. Children are very skillful at informing others that events from their past are being called forward into the present. Some of the common ways in which traumatic events are re-experienced include talking about the event as if it is happening in the present and/or frequently reminiscing about when it happened in the past. The major factor is that the recollection causes the child a significant level of distress. Recurring dreams about the event are another common way children re-experience traumatic events. Flashbacks (the child feels as if the traumatic event is happening again in the present) also serve to have children re-experience a traumatic event. Children may purposely re-enact the event in hopes of curtailing its recurrence in the future. A very common re-experiencing routine is for children to associate the traumatic event with an event, person, or situation. The associated object serves as a trigger and the child immediately feels as if the traumatic event is occurring again.

## Avoidance and Numbing

Deliberately limiting contact with a person, object, or circumstance that is associated with the traumatic event, an essential component of PTSD, constitutes avoidance. Limited contact includes physical contact as well as thoughts, feelings, and discussion that the child believes will reawaken the trauma for the victim. Sometimes the avoidance creates lapses of memory and the loss of developmental skills that were previously well-established. Short-term memory loss is a common example of avoidance that is observed among children with PTSD. Another prevalent symptom is the development of a sense of numbing, a pronounced decline of interest in responding to the external world. Detachment from others and an indifference to interpersonal relating are classic behaviors among children with PTSD where they feel that they are unable to connect with others. This position of isolation enhances their feelings of despair and gloom. When this occurs, children feel powerless in soliciting help from others.

## Hyperarousal

Persistent new symptoms of exaggerated response to their environment are necessary for a child to be diagnosed as having post-traumatic stress disorder. Concerns about safety and security are very pronounced. Startled reactions are common. Behavior not previously exhibited by the child (i.e. frequent temper outbursts, very poor attention span, overall irritability, impaired ability to stay focused on a task) is evidence of hyperarousal, and an important part of the clinical diagnosis for PTSD.

## Duration and Types

Many children exhibit several of the behavioral and cognitive symptoms of PTSD. However, the symptoms may be transient and disappear after a short time. Symptoms of PTSD are long-term and pervasive. Clinicians use the issue of severity and longevity of the child's behavior or experience to diagnose PTSD (Table 6.1).

## PTSD Children in the Classroom

Children who have PTSD are likely to exhibit an array of clinical symptoms in the classroom. Some symptoms will cause disruptions in the orderly flow of activities in the classroom while others will occur and are hardly noticed. The most important matter in trying to maintain a continuous relationship with children is awareness of abrupt changes in behavior. Such changes may be related to trauma the child has recently experienced. Mental health professionals and nurses in schools can be helpful in assessing for the presence of traumatic events and responses. Once children are diagnosed with PTSD, they are to continue with regular classroom instruction and social engagement. The routine treatment of disruptive behavior should continue in responding to children with PTSD. It is important not to make the child an example or to interrogate publicly. Such behavior will further traumatize the child and reduces the likelihood of sharing critical information about the trauma that was recently experienced.

Children who have been diagnosed with post-traumatic stress disorder are also likely to experience several challenges to learning in the classroom (poor

**TABLE 6.1** PTSD types and duration

| Longevity of symptoms | Diagnosis |
| --- | --- |
| Less than one month | Insufficient duration for PTSD diagnosis |
| Two to three months | Acute PTSD |
| Three to six months | Chronic PTSD |
| Symptoms appear more than six months after traumatic event | Delayed onset PTSD |

attention span, inability to concentrate, impulsivity, detachment from the current activities of the classroom, and sudden lapses into sadness). The most pronounced behavior is likely to be *detachment from the activities of the classroom*. The explanation for such behavior is that the trauma the child recently experienced interferes with mental processing ability. The trauma the child has experienced interferes with the ability to think about anything except the trauma. This interference becomes more pervasive when the child is unable to discuss the trauma with another person. The child is emotionally and mentally consumed by traumatic memories and becomes powerless to communicate feelings and thoughts. The process, however, does not occur without behavioral warnings such as blank stares into space, nonparticipation in routine classroom activity, and becoming non-responsive to the teacher and classmates.

Significant and frequent mood swings are classic symptoms for children with PTSD. To a casual observer, there is no apparent explanation for the change in affect. The responses to the child's sudden mood swing are often misunderstood and even ostracized by others. The mystery surrounding the emotional change is not so great. The trauma that the child experienced is triggering the mood swings. Developmentally, children have a limited emotional repertoire. Post-traumatic stress disorder further limits children's ability to respond. Anger, sadness, and fear are emotions that are frequently exhibited by children with PTSD. These emotions are usually in response to the trauma children have experienced and are reliving the experience in their brain, not in response to anything that is currently happening in their environment. The reliving of the trauma is very real to the child. It isolates the child from his or her own world of thoughts and feelings. The frequency and onset of mood swings varies unpredictably. The impact of such mood swings is very consistent in preventing the child from being "present" to engage in the behavioral and academic activities of the classroom. So, what is a teacher to do?

## Short Attention Span

A child's ability to attend to one task for a sustained period of time is partly a function of the child's age. Other features that influence attention span include the level of attractiveness of the task, frequency at which the child is engaged during the activity, and other competing environmental forces such as background noises and intensity of other activity. A plethora of factors have been cited in the developmental and educational literature as being contributors to short attention span in the classroom. Unfortunately, PTSD has not been prominently reflected in the literature. The dynamic between PTSD and short attention span is the same as the relationship between short attention span and other conditions. One critical difference is that most of the conditions have a longer history of being a recognized disorder in children than PTSD. This leads to the ongoing challenge of clinical practitioners and teachers' lack of knowledge about the symptoms of the disorder. Indeed, the common error of associating PTSD with adults and military combat is an ongoing problem. Among PTSD children, short attention span appears to be related to the cognitive blocking used to avoid memories of the trauma.

## Helping Children Deal with Post-Traumatic Stress Disorder

It is now accepted that children as young as preschoolers can have post-traumatic stress reactions similar to adults' and that persist for many months or years (Udwin, 1993). Schoolchildren may be exposed to trauma in their personal lives or increasingly at school. Classroom teachers can help prepare children to cope with trauma by understanding the nature of trauma, teaching children skills for responding to an emergency, and learning to mitigate the after-effects of trauma. Specifically, teachers can utilize the daily routines of the classroom to provide a safe and therapeutic environment for traumatized children. Academic activities can be adjusted to provide a special ambiance of acceptance that gently encourages traumatized children to participate in the classroom community and to avoid isolating behaviors that intensify the effects of the trauma.

Care should be exercised in identifying a child as having post-traumatic stress disorder. The diagnosis should only be determined by an appropriately trained mental health professional. On a practical level, many children experience events that, if uninterrupted, have the potential for being traumatic. Causes of trauma in school-aged children can be divided into three categories: intra-familial violence (e.g. experience of parental abuse, witness of parental violence, sexual abuse); extra-familial violence (e.g. school violence, sniper attack); and political violence (e.g. exposure to war) (Karcher, 1994). More recent episodes of mass shootings, including those in schools, killing of law enforcement officers, and high rates of violence and crime in the community contribute to trauma among school-aged children.

Again, a word of caution about making the logical connection between trauma and post-traumatic stress disorder. Not all emotionally upsetting experiences lead to post-traumatic stress disorder. Trauma sufficient to induce PTSD has specific characteristics and circumstances, including situations perceived as life-threatening, experiences during which the child loses control of the outcome, and when death is observed.

Classroom teachers should be actively involved in helping to identify and referring children suspected of being victims of traumatic events for mental health diagnostic and treatment services. One of the greatest challenges in helping children with emotional difficulties is related to reporting concerns to a mental health professional. This dilemma is especially true with regard to post-traumatic stress disorder. The tendency to use the term loosely is pervasive, and often leads to bigger and more complex problems for children, parents, and the school community. Underreporting of concerns leads to problems of a different type.

First, the longevity of exposure to trauma and violence is one dimension that should be assessed, and acute distinguished from chronic. Acute exposure refers to more recent exposure, and chronic denotes exposure that is ongoing and of long-standing duration. The implications for these distinctions are that children who are experiencing acute exposure to trauma, and perhaps warranting a diagnosis of PTSD, are likely to exhibit dramatic changes in behavior and academic performance in the classroom. They may have previously been performing in a satisfactory manner and then suddenly, and seemingly with no warning, exhibited a dramatic shift in behavior. Not completing classroom assignments, not returning homework, and significant changes in social interactions within the classroom are common symptoms of an acute episode. When questioned about such behavior, the child may not even be aware of the change in his or her presentation. Reports from parents can be helpful in such instances. The most critical part of helping the child should be direct engagement in dialogue about the observed changes. Take note of what the child offers as an explanation and how it is articulated. Children who have acute episodes of trauma frequently attempt to avoid talking about the situation or their reaction to it. Encouraging children to write about recent events in their lives has consistently proven useful in identifying events that need to be thoroughly investigated. Children who are experiencing trauma (including loss of parents) for sustained periods of time should be evaluated for chronic trauma. Reversing the effects of chronic trauma is challenging because it often becomes the "new norm" by which children and families evaluate their experiences. Chronic trauma and chronic PTSD interfere with a child's normal developmental process. For example, a child with lengthy exposures to parental separation because of employment or military service may become fearful of spending much time away from the residential parent. This type of fear can lead the child to forego opportunities for bonding with friends at school, through sleepovers, and extended school field trips. The child's fears may be accompanied by parents being overly protective and not encouraging the child to socialize beyond the boundaries of the family.

A second dimension of PTSD that may adversely affect the child in school is the inability to recall details of important social and learning activities. This pattern of behavior is one of the many symptoms that the clinician will use in establishing a diagnosis of PTSD. It is important for classroom teachers to consider the child's ability to recall details of important social and learning activities when assessing less than optimal performance during classroom activities. Often the trauma that is the basis of the child's PTSD blocks the capacity to retrieve historical information. The recalled events may trigger memory of the trauma itself. To prevent the recall of unwanted memories, the child may exhibit a lapse of memory for details of certain events from the past. Consider the common situation where a child witnessed others being hurt by acts of violence in the community. Recalling those events often intensifies feelings of fear and sadness. Left unprocessed, those feelings are likely to erupt, with no warning, and to impair the child's capacity for engaging in the normal social order of connecting with the classroom community. There are risks involved in inviting children to openly discuss losses and fears in a communal setting. However, the initial invitation to participate in group discussions of "things happening in the community" is a safe way of identifying events that are bothersome to students. Classroom writing assignments about issues such as loss, separation, and even death can help in this regard. With the help of a mental health professional, exercises in which children are asked to take the perspectives of persons on different sides of an issue can be very illuminating and of high diagnostic value.

A third PTSD behavior that may find expression in a classroom setting is an intense and exaggerated response to a seemingly minor offense. PTSD has a different developmental course depending on the age of the victim. The clinical expression of re-experiencing can vary across developmental span. Young children may report new onset of frightening dreams without content specific to the traumatic event. Before age 6, young children are more likely to express re-experiencing symptoms through play that refers directly or symbolically to the trauma. Children may focus on imagined interventions in their play or storytelling. In addition to avoidance, children may become preoccupied with reminders. Children may experience co-occurring traumas (e.g. physical abuse, witnessing domestic violence) and in chronic circumstances may not be able to identify onset of symptoms (DSM-V). Avoidance behavior may be associated with restricted play or exploratory behavior in young children. School-aged children may opt not to participate in normal school activities. Older children and adolescents may make themselves socially undesirable and become estranged from peers. The pattern of symptoms in PTSD produces different behavioral outcomes depending on the chronological and developmental age of the child.

The main point is that PTSD is the development of characteristic symptoms following exposure to one or more traumatic events. The disorder can occur at any age, with symptoms that usually begin within three months after the traumatic event. The patterns in symptoms are standard but may be expressed in any number of ways, depending on the skills and development of the traumatized individual.

## Depression

Depression is generally thought about from the perspective of an adult. There are similarities between adult expressions of depression and those of children, but there are also some important differences that compromise a child's learning capacity, limit their growth and development, and in extreme cases can lead to death. Within the context of this chapter, the attention is focused on depression as it appears in childhood and adolescence.

The term depression is used frequently and can refer to many different behavioral responses. It has been used to refer to a brief state of being sad and the reaction to a recent event. Other common terms for that type of being include sad, down in the dumps, and blue. In many daily situations of loss and/or disappointment, a reaction of depression is appropriate to the situation. Another usage of the term depression refers to a clinical diagnosis that is meant to convey the idea that an individual has a cluster of symptoms that collectively renders them to be at a less than optimal level of functioning. In extreme cases of depression, an individual may verbalize thoughts of harm to themselves (suicide) and may need to be hospitalized. Children can have all symptoms of depression, even as they attempt to go about daily activities at home and in school. Teachers can be very instrumental in helping to identify children who are having transient episodes of depression and those who are struggling with pervasive and intense episodes of depression that warrant hospitalization.

According to Martorin and Ruiz (2009), people who earlier in life were deprived and traumatized may be less resilient and more prone to chronic depression than others. Repeated failures and the impact of unrelenting, uncomfortable, and unpredictable negative life events may set the stage for learned helplessness in humans just as they do in animals (p. 1094). This is a powerful statement of forecasting that has implications for understanding the behaviors and attitudes of children and those of their parents and grandparents.

The most pronounced features of depression, whether as a brief state of being or a diagnosis of a more long-term condition, are sadness (i.e. flat affect), low energy, a lack of interest in things that at other times are the source of pleasure and excitement (i.e. anhedonia), and reported feelings of despair. Any or all of these features may be present at varying levels. More intense accumulation of symptoms results in behavioral and thought processes that make it apparent that the individual is troubled. The lower levels of symptoms that appear intermittently are more difficult to identify. Continuous low levels of depressive symptoms can seriously interfere with normal development and learning in educational settings. Identifying the more acute manifestations of depression is easier than identifying and assessing the presence and impact of the lower level of depression.

At a very basic level, depression presents in children and adults with many of the same symptoms. There are, however, differences in how the symptoms get expressed and viewed by the depressed person. One of the greatest differences in presentation is that most adults can verbalize their feelings. Children, on the other hand, often lack the language skills to spontaneously articulate their feelings and thoughts about how they are feeling. Rather, they are more likely to respond to questions from others about how they feel or wait for others to interpret their behavior as being problematic. Unlike adults, in many instances, children are unable to associate their feelings with recent events that have occurred in their lives. The dilemma of understanding early warning signs is made even more difficult in school settings because of the presence of other children. During the school day, a child is likely to display a limited repertoire of behaviors. That means problem behaviors may go unnoticed because opportunities for their display are limited. Similarly, depressed children are at risk for being overlooked because they are quiet and not engaging in behaviors that are disruptive in the classroom.

The outcomes associated with childhood depression are significant and may be costly for years into the future. Academic skills and subject matter knowledge may not be developed because a child does not pay attention or is not engaged on a regular basis. The reluctance to ask for help with a task may further delay a child's mastery of knowledge and skills. Depressed children tend to be isolated and alienated from their peers, sometimes causing delays in social maturation. Recently, there has been an increased fascination with electronic games and toys. Depressed children are prime candidates for seeking refuge from appropriate interpersonal interaction with peers and family members by losing themselves in games. Recently, the World Health Organization (Wilkinson, 2018) and the American Academy of Pediatrics (2017) have warned about electronic games and have suggested that "gaming" should be considered a mental disorder.

Children who display depressive behaviors are likely to engage in unusual behaviors at home and in other social settings. This reality provides a wonderful opportunity for school personnel to gather information from parents and family members in order to better understand the child's behavior across multiple settings. This cross-referencing provides a wonderful opportunity for school personnel to build a relationship with other systems in which the child functions. At the very least, it provides an opportunity for teachers to collaborate with families in devising action plans for children. So, what are concepts that teachers need to keep in mind as they consider the possibility that a child's atypical behavior in a classroom setting may be related to depression?

It is important to distinguish a depressive reaction to a recent event (i.e. loss of a friendship, poor performance on a school assignment) from a larger and more pervasive change (i.e. death of a family member, parental strife and conflict) whose effects linger beyond a few days. The former should be categorized as a depressive episode and the latter may warrant an extensive examination of a depressive disorder. Diagnoses should only be made by licensed healthcare providers who are familiar with developmental disorders of childhood and adolescence.

Depressive symptoms sometimes appear immediately following an event of disappointment and/or loss. That is a normal progression of events. Those same symptoms are also likely to go away after a short period of time, sometimes even though there are no special efforts for alleviation. In such instances, the person who was exhibiting depressive symptoms is thought of as returning to baseline functioning. No one and nothing are seriously impacted by such brief intermittent episodes. At the other end of the spectrum are the depressive symptoms that linger for extended periods of time and pose serious threats to the individual's ability to complete required daily activities, including school. The depressive symptoms continue to be present for an extended period, with increasingly disruptive impact on the affected person's life. When the symptoms linger, a diagnosis of depression should be considered. With regard to schoolchildren, the teacher and parents should seek the assistance of a mental health professional in deciding that a diagnosis of depression is warranted and that the symptoms are indeed persisting for an extended period of time. Two weeks of continuous depressive symptoms is sufficient time for a child to recover from a brief depressive episode. When the symptoms persist for a longer period, a diagnosis of depression should be considered.

The issue for teachers in this matter is being very observant of changes in a child's mood and behavior. It is, however, not enough to conclude that depressive symptoms are present by simply asking the child. Conversations with the child can reveal invaluable information about how the child is feeling and thinking. The child's inner psychological life (i.e. feelings, thoughts about self and the world) can be explored by talking with the child. The conversations don't have to be extensively probative, but can be a simple matter of factual inquiry about what the child did over the weekend or what the child plans to do after school. Valuable information is gained by noting the child's enthusiasm, or lack thereof, in talking about their activities. Also, rate of verbal response offers other important pieces of information about the presence or absence of depression. Slower than normal responses are usually a positive indicator that should be explored further. As the conversation with the child unfolds, the teacher might carefully inquire about explanations for things. Asking the child "Why?" will provide indication of the child's ability to explain things and of their understanding of relationships between events and people. In many instances where there is a strong sense of helplessness and despair, the "why" question is answered with "because" and nothing more. This suggests that the child is limited in language skills and/or the ability to convey information about feelings and thoughts.

The bottom line here is that a first line of inquiry should be whether the depressive symptoms observed are brief and respond to a recent event, or of intense and long duration. A two-week critical period is sufficient to consider symptoms as being long- or short-term.

Parents can be a valuable ally for teachers in seeking to verify the presence of depressive symptoms and their level of severity. The settings in which parents and teachers observe children in action are varied. It is dissimilarity that adds richness to the observations. For example, teacher observations of a child being unresponsive to instructional directions may add strength to a parent's similar observations about a child being unable to follow complex commands that may be given in the context of the home.

In order to enlist the parent's cooperation in collecting observations about a child's behavior, the teacher may invite the parent to "describe the child's behavior at home" rather than asking about specific behaviors. The latter has the effect of biasing the parent's report. Careful attention should be given to the fact that family relationships are of a longer duration and probably include more levels of complexity (i.e. sibling relations, parental relations, neighbors, etc.) than school relationships (i.e. teacher, classmates, children in other grades).

Ideally, information should be collected and compiled over a period of time to make sure there is a reasonable sample of behavior on which to base conclusions.

One very important issue in comparing data from parents with data from teachers is that parents are sometimes guarded about admitting that there are concerns about their child's behavior. Acknowledging that their child is struggling is sometimes inaccurately interpreted as an indictment of their parenting skills. To guard against this difficulty, the invitation to have the parent report about their child's behavior should not be accusatory or even suggestive that there is something "wrong." The child's behavior will be evaluated once data have been collected and analyzed.

### What Happens When the Data Are Collected and the Results Are Inconsistent?

A closer review of the data may reveal that the results are not as disparate as appeared at first glance. It could be a case of the observers having different views of the child. Different operational definitions of the target behavior that are reported might also explain the inconsistent results. When a difference of opinion is reached, it should be explored and the data from both sides should be considered as important. All data should be maintained and shared with the consulting mental health professional (i.e. school social worker, school psychologist).

### What Happens When the Frequency of Behaviors of Concern Vary Greatly?

The level of concern that a teacher has about a child's behavior can be influenced by the extent of disruption it causes within the classroom. The same can be said about parents who spend vast amounts of time with their child. Observations of children with symptoms of depression may be compromised because the child is not causing any noticeable disruption at home or at school. Children with symptoms of depression often exist silently in their own world of helplessness, sadness, and despair. Getting entry into the child's world through conversation is the most likely way of knowing and potentially understanding what the child is thinking and feeling. Sometimes that process is made more difficult because of feelings of shame and guilt that prevent the child from sharing openly. There is also the risk that the child will be careful not to disclose information that is so emotionally charged that they "can't tell anybody." The risk of nondisclosure can be overcome by the teacher carefully crafting instructional assignments that make it easier for the child to talk about her or his inner psychological life, real and imaginary. Both provide valuable insights into the child's world.

Verbal reports are a standard way of assessing children's behavior. Another domain for deciding whether depression is a possible factor in a child's life is to observe behavior. Slow movement and lack of energy (psychomotor retardation) are behavioral cues that the teacher should be especially mindful of observing. Sudden changes in the level of engagement a child has with siblings and class-mates are classic behaviors that help rule out depression as a current concern. The combination of behavioral observations and direct verbal reports provides strong evidence to support the hypothesis of depression that might warrant further clinical interventions.

All the foregoing information is intended to provide the classroom teacher with basic information regarding depression as a developmental issue that many students face. The greater challenge is how to translate that information into practical interventions that can be implemented efficiently and quickly. Basic questions that need to be answered when helping a child who is believed to be experiencing behavioral and/or emotional difficulties include the following: What are the pieces of evidence that lead the teacher to believe there is a problem? How reliable are the sources of data that suggest there is a problem? What is a reasonable plan of action for testing the hypothesis that there is a problem? Who will carry out the plan of action? What is the desired ultimate outcome?

## What Are the Pieces of Evidence That Lead the Teacher to Believe There Is a Problem?

Has there been a change in the student's pattern of behavior and learning that the teacher thinks is atypical? This includes grades received, the level of enthusiasm about completion of assignments, and the overall approach to participation in classroom activities. Changes in social interaction, such as spontaneous interactions with other students, should be noted. Irritability and isolation are frequently significant indicators of social-emotional difficulties. More overt signs such as crying and aggression toward others, without provocation, are major indicators that something is wrong and should be addressed immediately. The larger idea here is that the learning and growth that a child is likely to accomplish in school are affected by academic and social factors. Children in emotional distress and unrest are less likely to acquire and retain new knowledge. Teachers can confirm their observations and concerns by speaking with parents about any changes that they have observed in the recent past. Ideally, consultations with parents should be done in a routine manner by asking how the child is doing at home rather than sounding an alarm that "something is wrong." A compilation of teacher observations (concerns) and parental reports become the starting point for making a diagnosis and crafting an intervention strategy and timetable.

Once the teacher has evidence to support a belief that a child is in distress, a consultation should be held with support personnel in the school. The consultation should state the concerns as clearly as possible. If the teacher is wanting a formal evaluation of the child, it is necessary to have a specific referral question to ask the professional. Statements such as "I want him evaluated" without indicating the underlying question is less helpful than raising questions such as

"Is he depressed?" or "Does he have a learning disability?" Once the question is posed, it then becomes the responsibility of the person receiving the referral to decide how the question will be answered (i.e. classroom observations, review of academic performance records, formal psychological testing, etc.).

## Who Will Carry Out the Plan of Action?

The teacher initiating the action should be actively involved in making certain there is an explicit timetable for when answers to the questions will be forthcoming. In many school districts, there are clearly established guidelines for due dates of responses to requests regarding formal consultations and evaluations.

## What Is the Desired Outcome?

The goal of the intervention should be objective, measurable, and intelligible to all persons involved. The more specifically the goal can be stated, the better. Improved emotional functioning to increase the child's academic performance is the ultimate goal. A secondary goal of intervention is to improve the quality of services to a child and the family so that the child's performance reaches its highest potential and the circumstances that led to the intervention will not reoccur in the future.

One important part in planning for assessments and interventions is avoiding unnecessary attention to the child and the family. Sometimes heightened attention has the effect of improving performance simply because the child is aware of being observed (Hawthorne effect). The phenomenon has been demonstrated in work settings and in academic environments. A useful strategy where students are sensitive to emotional interferences is to observe and document behavior at various times during the day and under different circumstances at home.

## What Does This Mean for Attending to the Needs of Depressed Children in the Context of the Classroom?

Children with emotional disturbances who are continuously unavailable have difficulty receiving and internalizing information. Negative feelings interfere with the encoding of new information because information-processing circuits of the brain cannot synthesize additional material. When the brain is exposed to more information than it can process, the child responds negatively or fails to respond. The latter is demonstrated by depressed children who ignore new stimuli altogether by falling asleep (an extreme example) or appear to be distracted.

After the teacher has identified a child exhibiting symptoms of emotional issues, the child should be referred to the support personnel for specialized assistance. Usually, the child who is identified as struggling with emotional issues is already detached from activities in the classroom. Further isolation increases feelings of being different and detached. Instead, the assessment can be completed in the classroom setting. Use of the familiar environment can enhance the child's feelings of safety and confidence. This may even normalize the assessment and intervention process. This inclusion approach increases the possibility of capturing aspects of the child's best possible performance. The child's performance that cannot be observed and documented in the regular classroom, under usual circumstances, should be completed in the office of the supporting professionals.

The discussion so far has focused on PTSD and depression and the impact on the emotional life of school-aged children. Practices have been presented that will help teachers monitor the behavior of children with these specific clinical conditions. Based on the data presented here, the teacher is a collaborating professional who plays a critical role in making certain that children with special emotional needs get appropriate attention. The next section will discuss strategies that can be applied for effectively engaging children with emotional and behavioral disorders in classroom learning. The goal for these practices is to simultaneously equip students to cope with dissonant emotions and empower them to pursue higher-order thinking and learning. At the end of the section, there is a review of pedagogical practices that have been empirically shown to have the greatest benefit in helping children with emotional and behavioral disorders.

## Strategies for Teaching Emotional and Behavioral Disordered Children

### Mathematics

Camenzuli and Baghiar (2014) advocate the use of inquiry-based learning (IBL) in the teaching of mathematics to students with social, emotional, and behavioral difficulties (SEBD). In their study, subjects were 13 male students in secondary school. Several sources of data were utilized, including teacher observations that were recorded in a reflective journal and two sessions of in-depth interviews with students. Journal writings by students along with samples of students' work and school-based half-yearly and annual mathematics examinations were also included. Findings from the yearlong project suggest that the use of IBL in the mathematics classroom can benefit students with SEBD in a number of ways, including but not limited to a sense of enjoyment during learning experiences, improved student behavior and motivation to learn, and facilitating the learning of mathematics. A slightly different approach to discovering the optimal approach to teaching mathematics to SEBD children was employed by Billingsley, Scheurermann, and Webber (2009). They wanted to answer the question of which of three instructional methods was most effective in teaching mathematics to secondary students with emotional and behavioral disorders. Direct teaching, computer-assisted instruction, and a combination of the two methods were used. No one method was consistently superior to the others. However, the combined methods were more effective for some learners. Variables such as number of years in school, medical conditions, and attendance and motivation were found to have a significant effect on learning outcomes.

Ralston, Benner, Tsai, Riccomini, and Nelson (2014) utilized a best-evidence synthesis of the effects of mathematical instruction on the mathematics skills of students with emotional and behavioral disorders in a review of research dating back over four decades (1968 to present). Fifty-four studies were reviewed. Two notable findings in that literature are that direct or explicit instruction is effective in building conceptual understanding and basic mathematics skills, and that the majority of the mathematics interventions are related to self-regulation (Ralston et al., 2014, p. 2). Despite the clarity of these findings, it still has not been established what specific instructional or intervention components contributed most to student responsiveness. One conclusion of the synthesis is that there are interventions and supports that can help combat mathematical deficits that are often found among emotional and behavioral disordered children. These approaches include peer-mediated strategies such as peer tutoring and peer-assisted learning strategies. Other effective approaches include self-mediated strategies, including self-regulated strategy development and cover, copy, compare. Pedagogical approaches such as direct instruction and constant time delay were effective.

## Language Arts

Hauth, Mastropieri, Scruggs, and Regan (2013) explored the teaching of emotional and behavioral disordered children in the area of language arts. They used a multiple-baseline design to examine the effects of teaching persuasive writing and applying writing in the civics content area. A self-regulated strategy development (SRSD) was utilized in combination with a teaching intervention. Pre- and post-testing were completed. According to the researchers, all students improved substantially on all essay measures, including essay length, essay quality, and number of essay parts, sentences, and paragraphs. Eight emotional and behavioral disordered eighth graders participated in the study. Conclusions based on the study are that EBD children have the capacity to make significant progress in the areas of writing and civics. Similar conclusions were reached by Datchuck, Kubina, and Mason (2015) after their study of elementary-aged students in a single case experimental design study with behavioral disorders and learning disabilities. Sentence construction was combined with practice procedures. Overall, students produced gains in the frequency of simple sentences constructed.

Garwood, Brunsting, and Fox (2014) examined the question of effectiveness in teaching reading skills to EBD children by reviewing the professional literature in that area. They completed a systematic review of comprehension and fluency approaches for middle and high school students served outside of the general education classroom since 2004. Nine studies were analyzed. All studies utilized a single-subject design and contained a variety of practices.

Losinski, Cuenca-Carolina, Zalocki, and Teagarden (2014) note that self-regulated strategy instruction is an evidence-based practice that can improve the writing skills of students with emotional and behavioral disorders. Their meta-analysis of 20 studies indicated that self-regulated strategy instruction (SRSD) had large effect sizes across three dependent variables (i.e. essay elements, quality, and word count). Type of instruction, intervention agent, and gender did not significantly predict response to SRSD instruction. Another meta-analysis reported by Benner, Nelson, Ralston, and Mooney (2010) suggests that effective literacy instruction has a positive effect on the reading skills of students with or at risk for behavioral disorders. Both studies conclude that emotional and behavioral disordered children can respond positively to various methods of instruction. Other than SRSD, noted in the Losinski et al. (2014) study, no specific teaching approach to reading is noted as being superior to others.

Additional support for the use of self-regulatory approaches to bolster readiness for learning and improvements in level of performance is found in the work of Young-Pelton and Bushman (2015). They examined the effectiveness of a video self-modelling intervention with school-aged children ($n = 4$) who attended a full-time special education program for students with social and emotional behavioral difficulties and who exhibited inappropriate behavior during small group reading instruction. The 10-year-old students were videotaped to determine levels of active learning and behavioral difficulties. During the experimental intervention, the children were shown carefully selected segments of their own video that had been recorded during the previous session. Results indicated that video self-modeling (VSM) was an effective intervention for increasing active learning engagement and for reducing behavioral difficulties during reading instruction. Behavioral changes were sustained for at least eight weeks, supporting the author's contention that VSM is an effective approach.

## Gang Affiliation

Popular conceptions about gangs and their dynamics have contributed to failure in developing effective assessment and intervention strategies to assist gang members in becoming healthy and productive members of society. Much of the incomplete information on gangs seems to be related to media portrayals—the lack of understanding of ethnic and cultural components of some gangs is a prime example. In some neighborhoods, gangs have existed as a part of the social fiber of the community for generations, with a coexistence of gang and non-gang actions. The lack of knowledge about the history of gangs in particular neighborhoods leads to overwhelmingly negative interpretations and the desire for their destruction. Yet these gangs may serve important social functions for the community or they may become objects of projection, a convenient group for the community to loathe (Branch, 1999, p. 4).

The literature on adolescent gangs has heavily focused on issues of juvenile delinquency and crime. Researchers have been less interested in underlying psychiatric dynamics that give rise to gang membership or the psychiatric dynamics and mental status of gang members. For example, the issues of how gang members relate to the hierarchy of the gang's organizational structure has been discussed by scholars and researchers investigating the operation of gangs. The more intimate dynamics of what happens at the level of individuals (i.e. cognitive processes that give rise to behaviors, etc.) have not been extensively explored. Even the idea of conversion from normative to gang membership has received little coverage in the professional literature. Perhaps one of the most obvious and costly oversights has been the systematic investigation of gang members in schools. The literature on gangs within schools has been focused mostly on issues of violence, delinquency, and safety that arise from gang members within school communities. It appears to me that a more interesting and complex issue is the challenges teachers and other school personnel face with gang members in schools. Is the major challenge to isolate and neutralize the disruptive impact of identifiable gang members in a school? Is the main goal to convince gang members to leave the gang? Is the main goal to disrupt the transition of non-gang members to the status of being a "gangsta"? How are pedagogy and learning influenced by gang members in the classroom?

Very little has been written about what teachers do to ensure learning for all students, including those who profess to be gang members or are in the process of becoming a gang member. Are there best practices that are found to be effective with gang members and those in the process of becoming? The first issue in the school community is the knowledge that teachers and others have about gangs and gang membership. Branch (1999) notes that the definitional dilemma relative to gangs is considerable. Various definitions have been offered over time that reflect the interests of those generating the definitions. Thrasher (1927) conceptualized a gang as an interstitial group, originally founded spontaneously and then integrated through conflict. In this conceptualization, gangs are characterized by such behavior as meeting face-to-face, milling, movement through space as a unit, conflict, and planning. The result of this collective behavior is the development of tradition, unreflective internal structure, *esprit de corps*, solidarity, morale, group awareness, and attachment to a local territory (Thrasher, 1927, cited in Jankowski, 1991, p. 3). Thrasher's words have formed the foundation for many subsequent definitions, each stressing different elements of the gang's existence. A few examples of the range of definitions are presented in Table 6.2.

The issue of gang intervention has received a high level of attention from criminologists, sociologists, and educators. Each group of practitioners and scholars have debated the merits of one approach over another. The issue of defining a gang and the implications for developing appropriate interventions has been reviewed by several scholars.

**TABLE 6.2** Definition of a gang

---

Miller (1974): A youth gang is a self-formed association of peers, bound together by
mutual interests, with identifiable leadership, well-developed lines of authority,
and other organizational features, who act in concert to achieve a specific purpose,
which generally includes the conduct of illegal activity and control over a particular
territory, facility, or type of enterprise.

Huff (1993): Youth gang—A collectivity consisting primarily of adolescents and
young adults who (a) interact frequently with one another; (b) are frequently and
deliberately involved in illegal activities; (c) share a common collective identity that is
usually, but not always, expressed through a gang name; and (d) typically express that
identity by adopting certain symbols or claiming control over certain "turf" (persons,
places, things, or economic markets).

Huff (1993): Organized crime gang—A collectivity consisting primarily of adults who
(a) interact frequently with one another; (b) are frequently and deliberately involved
in illegal activities directed toward economic gain, primarily through the provision
of illegal goods and services; and (c) generally have better defined leadership and
organizational structure than is found in a youth gang.

Fagan (1996): Research conducted by Fagan during the 1980s identified two types of
gangs: party gangs that were mainly involved in drinking and drugs, as well as drug
sales, and social gangs that used drugs and committed numerous petty crimes. He also
found other gang types (delinquent gangs, young organizations) that resembled the
territorial and corporate gangs described by Taylor (1990).

---

Esbensen, Winfree, He, and Taylor (2001) explored the question of youth
gangs and the definitional dilemma directly in a study of 6,000 middle school
students. They devised a range of definitions of gangs, from no restrictions
("includes everyone who claims to be a gang member") to highly restrictive ("only
those youth who are current core gang members who indicate that their gang has
some degree of organizational structure and whose members are involved in illegal
activities") (p. 105). Esbensen et al. (2001) highlight the dilemma of over- versus
underestimating the prevalence of gangs and the effect of such gangs on public
perceptions and the development of policies for implementation: "Clearly, the definitions of gang membership used by researchers and policy makers have important
implications for both research results and the ways policy makers employ these
findings" (p. 107). Educators are included in that category of policymakers. Are
gangs treated as a sociopathic entity that exists in the bowels of urban communities
only, or do they also thrive within the confines of educational institutions? If the
latter is true, what are the implications for educators?

An understanding of the pervasiveness and impact of gangs on communities
will help increase appreciation for the seriousness of the issue, as will recognizing
that gangs (restrictively or nonrestrictively defined) influence safety in communities and schools. Perhaps more importantly, an understanding of gangs can

help teachers examine and review their own attitudes about teaching the diverse students in a classroom.

The definitional dilemma is further exacerbated when educators are confronted with the reality that gangs exist within urban communities, including schools. Gangs also exist within suburban communities! Acceptance of the last proposition usually requires a rethinking of one's assumption that gangs are an exclusively inner-city problem. The idea that gang members operate and thrive within schools is also a new and difficult reality for many people to internalize. However, all the foregoing findings are true and have been empirically verified.

Gangs in the context of schools are usually reported in relation to the issue of school violence (Curry, 2000; Estrada, Gilrealth, Astor, & Benbenishty, 2013; Gottfredson, Gottfredson, & Wiseman, 2001; Nabor, May, Decker, Minor, & Wells, 2006). The issue of violence in schools and gangs is not a simple and straightforward matter. Generic beliefs about the relationship between the two issues have been refuted by Estrada and associates (Estrada et al., 2013; Estrada, Gilbreath, Astor, & Benbenishty, 2014; Estrada, Huerta, Hernandez, Hernandez, & Kim, 2018). Historic theory has created a belief that gangs are the cause of spikes in school violence. Detailed empirical research by Estrada et al. has shown that there is not a direct link between gang membership and school violence perpetration and victimization. Rather, they have discovered that the relations between gang membership and school violence perpetration and victimization were completely mediated by school risk behaviors and attitudes:

> Therefore, this study suggests that gang involvement alone does not result in school violence; however, when a gang-involved youth participates in school risk factors, such as truancy, substance use, and associating with risky peers, the probability of school perpetration and victimization can increase.
>
> *(Estrada et al., 2013, p. 637)*

This introduces the issue of how teachers should respond to the reality of gangs in school. A safe and non-risky reaction might dictate that the issue of gangs is not openly talked about. Behaving in such a way quells the anxiety of those who are "frightened" by the reality, and it also provides an illusion of safety and security, even while teachers and students privately struggle with their feelings about the issue. At a most basic level, this type of behavior can be characterized as a form of denial (i.e. not accepting as true a matter that can be objectively verified as being true).

Thinking of gang members only in the context of school violence is also a simple way of attending to a complex matter. Students who are gang members and are in the school community have the same learning and emotional needs as non- gang members. Teachers are required to respond to multiple needs (i.e. health, social, learning) that students have while they are attending school. This inclusivity extends

**TABLE 6.3** Gang membership classification and affiliation

| Classification | Affiliation |
| --- | --- |
| Level I: Fantasy identification with gang | Beginning psychological connection to a gang |
| Level II: At risk of gang involvement | Attracted to gang lifestyle, not participating |
| Level III: Wannabe/associate gang member | Ready to join a gang |
| Level IV: Gang member | Follow gang members, not hardcore |
| Level V: Hardcore gang member | Fully submerged personal and collective goals of gang membership |

to gang-affiliated students as well. Much has been written about interventions for gang-affiliated students and gangs. One of the major difficulties with a significant part of the literature is that gang interventions are often based on stereotypic images. Additionally, interventions with gang members are frequently focused on the violence and delinquency dimension, with no regard for other aspects of their lives, such as academic learning needs, social development, and growth and development as community residents.

Frequently, gang interventions are planned with the sole and express purpose of rescuing gang members from the gang. There have been celebrated attempts to create programs that will compete with the allure of gang affiliation without thinking critically about the process or the anticipated outcome. Gangs, like other groups, have a developmental course. Boys & Girls Clubs of America (1993) devised a classification scheme that codifies levels of gang members and affiliation. The value of it or any other classification scheme is that it assists the observer in determining how immersed in gang life and culture the gang member may be, as well as the "type" (i.e. level of dangerousness) that is attached to the affiliation.

According to the Boys & Girls Clubs of America (1993) classification, there are at least five levels of gang membership (Table 6.3).

The levels of membership and affiliation have implications for the types of gang activity for individuals. Perhaps just as important as the level of gang membership is the matter of type of gang. Esbensen et al. (2001) provide a detailed description of gangs that are loosely structured and are only minimally disruptive to members and the community. At the other end of the spectrum are highly lethal and toxic gangs that routinely participate in dangerous and illegal activities. It is necessary for an observer such as a teacher or other school personnel to be knowledgeable about the level of engagement of a student before attempting to devise an intervention.

Gaining information about a student's social and emotional connections that extend beyond the classroom can be a daunting task. Information can be obtained from the student directly and other parts of it can be gathered by interviewing others about the student. The most essential questions in this complex array of data sources are why a child wants to join a gang and how a teacher can be of assistance in guiding the child.

The question of why a student wants to be a member of a gang is at the heart of understanding the value of the gang to a student. What does the gang provide that is not provided to the student otherwise, real or imaginary? The appeal of gangs is often difficult for adults to understand. When asked to explain the attractiveness of gang membership, young people offer a plethora of reasons, many of which relate to psychological needs. The big challenge in helping gang-affiliated students is to hear and understand their explanation for joining the gang. Reasons students give for joining gangs include "safety in the community," "status in the neighborhood," "peer pressure," and being "connected to others" ("they are my family"). Other frequently verbalized reasons include "taking back turf," "gaining respect," and for political and social reasons. Branch (1999) noted that:

> Despite the absence of a consistent set of reasons for joining and remaining in gangs, membership in a gang does meet a need. The need itself may not be obvious to the gang member in a way that he or she can discuss openly with an "outsider". Rather, youth know that they feel good about being in the gang, but may not be able to explain what they receive from the gang.
>
> *(p. 198)*

One of the first struggles for teachers is often to accept the students' reasons for joining a gang as legitimate and real to the person sharing information. The presence of gang members in school communities poses several challenges and dilemmas for teachers. Perhaps the first problem is for teachers to make a quick review of what they know about gangs and how the knowledge was acquired. Many people, including teachers, never have any fact-based knowledge about gangs and gang members. Instead, they have notions of gang life presented in the media. Those portrayals come to be the basis for personal beliefs. In an ideal situation, a teacher may be inclined to carefully reflect on the accuracy of knowledge about gangs and whether it is likely to be helpful in making decisions about how to relate to or interact with a gang member. The reality of daily living, however, is that initial awareness of a student's gang affiliation is not likely to come in a relaxed moment of reflection.

Some reported gang members may really be level I (fantasy identification), level II (at risk), or level III (wannabe members). They may claim to be a part of a gang but they are not. Conversely, there may be level IV and level V gang members who are using the school setting as a recruitment station for the gang. Some gang members have reported that they have frequently used school buildings as a platform to carry out the program of the gang and at the same time avoid surveillance and apprehension by the police. So, encountering gang members in school communities is not as much of an anomaly as it might appear.

## *Are There Evidence-Based Teaching or Behavior Management Strategies That Can Be Employed to Help Gang Members Have a Stimulating and Useful Experience in School?*

This issue can be better understood by reflecting on the situation in a slightly different way. The task is finding ways to engage students that will lead to a good educational and social outcome. The educational outcome is learning and the internalization of knowledge and skills. Gang-affiliated students at various levels of gang engagement display behaviors, as do depressed and traumatized students, that can be challenging to teachers. Helping teachers recognize these behaviors requires a more than casual knowledge of students' life issues that may affect learning. Changing the primary social network can produce feelings of anxiety (i.e. poor ability to concentrate consistently) and depression (i.e. loss of loved objects and persons). When there are dramatic shifts in social relatedness, there are likely to be equivalent shifts in ability to sustain attention for extended periods of time. Both anxiety and depression are classic symptoms among students who are recently aligned with street gangs. Consulting with a counselor or school psychologist can help the teacher better understand the relationship between emotional stability and academic performance in school-aged children.

One educational approach that should be considered during the information-gathering stage of decision-making is whether a student is experiencing emotional difficulties that interfere with learning in individual or group work. This refers to having the child complete several assignments independently and then complete several similar assignments in a group context. Does isolating the child impact her or his level of anxiety and confidence? It is difficult to identify the source of a youngster's emotional angst without doing extensive information-gathering. However, the more quickly the preliminary assessment is completed, the more quickly the teacher can decide if the situation warrants more detailed evaluation by another type of professional. What is a teacher to do if the available information suggests that a student may be targeted for gang membership or has already become an active gang member?

## Gang-Affiliated Behaviors Impacting Academic Performance

A progressive view of the role of teachers includes addressing social and emotional issues as well as intellectual and cognitive development. Paying attention to who and what a student is interacting with outside of the school community is a sure way of monitoring social growth and development. What should a teacher do when she or he becomes aware of a student's participation in organized gang activities? The most logical answer is to gather information for making a well-informed decision about how to meet the student's needs. There may be needs that extend beyond the role and expertise of the teacher. If so, other professionals should be consulted and engaged in developing a comprehensive intervention plan for the student. After an intervention is developed and implemented, the student is still in the classroom and needs to be taught. The teacher should consider following four questions in preparing how to respond to a gang-affiliated student's classroom learning.

### Does the Student Show Evidence of Being More Detached and Distant from Others Than Previously?

Changes in emotional availability in the direction of becoming more withdrawn and detached from others is often a sign of depression. Children and adolescents are as likely to become depressed as are adults. Earlier in this chapter, it was pointed out that a distinction should be made between brief transient states of depression in response to an emotional setback and depressive disorders. The latter is more likely to be longer in duration and cause greater challenges for returning to a previous level of functioning. In the context of gang-affiliated students, brief episodes of depression are common as a transition is made from one identity status (pre-gang membership) to another (hardcore gang member). It appears that the depression is a reaction to the transition from the social world that was once primary to the uncertainty of a new identity as a gang member. This is somewhat surprising because the gang affiliation status was a desired goal. In some ways, young people who are in this type of transition are "in between" selves. School may be the one consistent space in the new gang member's life. Rather than appreciate and enjoy school, the new recruits may react with ambivalence in the form of withdrawal and sadness. The challenge, then, for the classroom teacher becomes how to discern that the student is indeed in transition and how to disrupt the student's slow detachment from the social environment of the classroom. Such teacher efforts are usually met with anger and hostility toward the teacher and fellow students.

### Does the Student Lack the Ability to Engage in Cooperative/ Reciprocal Social Exchanges with Others?

This indicator of a change is more than merely being detached from others. It is an expression of an inability to respond appropriately to social exchanges that are directed toward the student. From the perspective of an observer, it looks like unprovoked anger and hostility. Many new recruits to gangs and other organizations see the world through the eyes of their organization. It is akin to what happens with individuals who have major identity conversion experiences. They see themselves and their comrades as the only way to be. Everyone else is perceived as "the enemy" or at the very least "outsiders" who should not be tolerated. In the context of school, the learning environment and the knowledge or skills being taught are also attack and reject. Questioning the behavior is likely to intensify the anger and hostility. Listening carefully to the student's responses to questions about her or his behavior will provide further insights into the emerging blind acceptance of the rhetoric that is associated with the gang. References to "family" and not being understood by teachers and others are often heard. Perhaps the most useful piece of information that can be gleaned from inquiries about the student's recent behavior is that the arguments are often illogical. In many ways, they could be thought of as being gang-centric. Asking the student about their behavior results in extolling the virtues of the gang or their friends, as opposed to talking about and explaining their own behavior. This pattern of us versus them is frequently observed when new gang members suddenly become polarized in their expression of racial and ethnic attitudes. The shift to seeing the world through primarily militant racial and ethnic eyes invariably echoes the sentiments of the gang with which the student recently aligned herself or himself.

### Does the Student Have Short-Term Memory Lapses That Interfere with the Capacity to Complete Assignments?

Short attention span can be a symptom of any number of syndromes. Students who demonstrate an inability to stay focused on academic learning are often not invited to share what they are thinking about. Rather, they are often admonished to stay on task. In situations where the problem becomes chronic, there is usually an unmistakable reason for the "daydreaming" and "avoidance" of academic engagement. Depression is sometimes identified as a cause for the shift of attention. In the vocabulary of many students, learning experience is "boring," meaning the activity or topic does not capture their imagination. This situation should be observed to determine if it is evidence of a more serious problem. Individuals who are involved in major identity shifts (non-gang member to gang member) are a high risk for romanticizing their new identity, even at the expense of their current functioning. In some ways, the new identity preoccupies their thinking.

Developmentally, children are inclined to engage in binary or dichotomous thinking (either this or that). That is, things and people in their lives are good or bad, desirable or undesirable, and important or unimportant. The dichotomous thinking leads to an intense re-examination of where they should invest emotional energy. The task of deciding how to expend their energy includes the serious decision of what is worthy of attention and what is not. When engaged in the process of assuming a new identity, only things that are directly identifiable with the new identity are deemed to be important. In the case of young people seeking after the romanticized identity of becoming a "gangsta," only thoughts about that matter.

When the pattern of not paying attention occurs repeatedly and in a variety of school settings, the behavior should be systematically examined. Asking a student to talk about what they last remember is a good starting point for further evaluation. The lapse of attention and memory problems can be indications of more serious problems. The problems could be organic (i.e. brain pathology) or they could be functional (i.e. emotional). The cause of the interference is just as important as the fact that it is occurring. A welcoming and supportive conversation with the student about what has occurred will hep decrease inattentive and poorly focused behaviors on the child's part. The real cue to gathering information that will have pedagogical value is to remain neutral and accepting of whatever a student offers as an explanation for the memory and attention lapse. Again, the services of a mental health professional in assessing the severity of the memory and attention problem should be considered.

## Has the Student's Style of Responding to Teachers and Other School Authority Figures Changed Recently? How?

Gang-affiliated young people often have rigid and concrete styles of relating to and interacting with perceived authority figures. The organizational hierarchy of the gang with which they are affiliated is responded to with a high level of deference and allegiance. By contrast, adults and their perceived powers are approached with disdain and contempt. A similar dichotomous manner of responding to others is often observed among many adolescents. However, it is especially strong among gang-affiliated adolescents who are new to the gang. For them, an intensely negative response to outsiders (i.e. non-gang members) is a direct statement of how strongly the gang member identifies with the gang and its program. Rejection of others further symbolizes the gang members' movement away from the values and behaviors of the community they left when they joined the gang. The anger and hostility that surround the new gang may appear suddenly. Recipients of the aggressive behavior are likely to be startled by the appearance of the behaviors and their intensity. Teachers are at high risk for negative interaction because they represent dimensions of the pre-gang identity that is demoted to a level of irrelevance and unimportance once the gang affiliation is complete.

Another extreme variation on this negative emotional response pattern is selective mutism. It is a pattern in which the listener voluntarily becomes mute when questioned about certain topics. The psychiatric literature shows that in this syndrome, the listener chooses when to respond and when not to respond. Even when they are non-responsive, they hear the speaker but choose to respond with an unintelligible verbalization. Selective mutism in the context of discussing gang affiliation is an act of defiance and aggression, often meant to devalue the speaker and the topic that they are presenting. In more extreme cases, selective mutism may be the result of organic impairment (i.e. brain damage), but such is rarely the case with gang-affiliated students who are attending school.

Disturbances in mood regulation are common in many disorders that occur among children and adolescents. Gang affiliation is a special case of clinical symptoms suddenly appearing in students who previously appeared asymptomatic. A careful look at the student, however, will show that the symptoms gradually appeared, perhaps so slowly that the teacher hardly noticed them.

## Summary and Conclusions

*Teachers play a vital role in the lives of children who are impaired in their ability to have a meaningful experience at school because of emotional difficulties.* In addition to the fundamental role of helping children develop basic academic competencies, teachers are expected to be intimately involved in helping to identify children who may have special needs. The range of emotional issues that may interfere with learning and appropriate growth and development is considerable. Many of the problems that children exhibit in school are externalized, and as such are easier to identify. Also, there are problem behaviors that are internalized (i.e. depression), and as a result are more difficult to manage. In some instances, the internalized thoughts and feelings make identification difficult. For purposes of illustration, three internalizing disorders have been chosen for discussion in this chapter. They are presented separately here, but they often occur in tandem.

Depression is a disorder that is most frequently associated with adults rather than children and adolescents. There is, however, overwhelming evidence that depression, as an ongoing mood disorder and a transient state of being, can be found in individuals as young as preschool years. The critical difference between adults and children with depression is that the latter have fewer resources for expressing their thoughts and feelings. In the context of the school, children with depression are easily identified because of their flat affect and overall lethargic presentation. Behavioral indicators that a child is experiencing depression usually include inability to complete complex tasks, loss of interest in previously favored activities, and an overall limited connection to the environment (people and things).

Post-traumatic stress disorder was originally identified among military veterans who participated in combat. More recently, the disorder has been observed to occur in non-combat situations and to affect children and adults. The most salient feature of the disorder is that the victim continues to relive the trauma long after the event has ended. Memories of the trauma intrude on the victim's present functioning with regularity, but with unpredictable frequencies. PTSD among children is presented very differently than it is among adults. The one common feature in both age groups is that the traumatic event continues to be very real to the victim. Disruptions in social relations and capacity to internalize new information are hallmarks of PTSD among children. Caution should be exercised in assuming that any exposure to a traumatic event will result in long-term psychological damage. Sometimes a dangerous and life-threatening event may impinge on cognitive and emotional functioning of a student and result in continuing difficulties. Acute stress disorders may also occur after exposure to an event involving physical harm or threat to life in which the person's response involved intense terror, horror, or hopelessness. A clinically trained professional should be consulted to make a diagnosis of post-traumatic stress disorder.

Gang affiliation is different from depression and PTSD in that it is a self-created state. The child who joins a gang actively generates a host of post-joining issues that have psychological and safety concerns for themselves and others. Unlike depression and PTSD, gang affiliation is not a condition that has been subject to rigorous psychological study. There is no evidence-based treatment that has been shown to be effective in treating it. Rather, it is a lifestyle choice that can potentially alter the quality of a child's life.

Depression is frequently a common factor in many psychology syndromes that impair the functioning of school-aged children. The presence of depression is a likely predictor of more severe behaviors and outcomes. For example, depression among school-aged children frequently interrupts their opportunities for developing and sustaining age-appropriate relationships with peers. Depressed children are also likely to complain of physical ailments at a rate higher than non-depressed children. Not surprisingly, children who are depressed will present special needs in the classroom (i.e. not completing assignments, excessive absenteeism, low energy, sleeping in class). Teachers can be helpful in planning interventions for children who appear to be depressed in several ways. First, noting a change in the child's usual level and quality of behavior will be helpful in deciding if a full psychological evaluation is necessary. Talking with the child about the results of the observational data will serve the purpose of building an alliance with the child. Most depressed individuals are willing, even eager, to talk with others about what troubles them. Children and adolescents are no different in this regard. Special care should be taken to elicit specifics about the matters that the child may share about her or his condition. Vague references to offending events and people have the effect of further strengthening the power of the offending thing over the child's sense of personal agency. Calling the name of the offending thing gives the depressed person power, even power to overcome the thing. Finally, it should be remembered that depression that is more than a brief transient episode (i.e. a friend moved away) may be indicative of a larger and more deeply engrained problem. Other school personnel, such as a psychologist or nurse, should be consulted if the teacher believes a child is depressed and the situation does not get better in a few days. Depression that is deemed to be indicative of a larger and more severe situation should be referred to a medical practitioner for further evaluation and treatment. Teachers can make a unique contribution to helping identify depressed students by paying close attention to the quality of their academic work and noting any sudden and dramatic shifts in the quality of the work.

Perhaps the greatest challenge facing teachers who are charged with helping students who are not available emotionally and cognitively is to devise teaching and learning strategies that are evidenced-based and resistant to the disconnections that have been presented in this chapter. The pedagogical research presented here has shown that emotional and behavioral disordered children can learn and grow in the same manner as other children. The literature has not been so specific as to match psychiatric disorders with effective teaching strategies, but the possibilities are emerging.

## References

American Academy of Pediatrics (2017, November). Internet gaming disorder in children and adolescents. *Journal of Pediatrics*, 140 (Supplement 2), S81–S85. doi:10.1542/peds.2016-1758H.

Benner, G. J., Nelson, J. R., Ralston, N. C., & Mooney, P. (2010). A meta-analysis of the effects of reading instruction on the reading skills of students with or at risk of behavioral disorders. *Behavioral Disorders*, 35(2), 86–102.

Billingsley, G., Scheurermann, B., & Webber, J. (2009). A comparison of three instructional methods for teaching math skills to secondary students with emotional/behavioral disorders. *Behavioral Disorders*, 35(1), 4–18.

Boys & Girls Clubs of America (1993). *Targeted outreach to youth at risk of gang involvement: A prevention approach*. New York: Anchor.

Branch, C. (1999). *Adolescent gangs: Old issues, new approaches*. New York: Routledge.

Camenzuli, J. & Buhagiar, M. A. (2014). Using inquiry-based learning to support the mathematical learning of students with SEBD. *International Journal of Emotional Education*, 6(2), 69–85.

Curry, G. D. (2000). Self-reported gang involvement and officially recorded delinquency. *Criminology*, 38, 1253–1274.

Datchuck, S. M., Kubina, R. M., & Mason, L. H. (2015). Effects of sentence instruction and frequency building to a performance criterion on elementary-aged students with behavioral concerns and EBD. *Exceptionality*, 23(1), 34–53.

Esbensen, F., Winfree, L., He, N., & Taylor, T. (2001). Youth gangs and definitional issues: When is a gang a gang, and why does it matter? *Crime and Delinquency*, 47(1), 105–130.

Estrada, J. N., Gilbreath, T., Astor, R., & Benbenishty, R. (2013). Gang membership of California middle school students: Behaviors and attitudes as mediators of school violence. *Health Education Research*, 28(4), 626–639.

Estrada, J. N., Gilbreath, T., Astor, R., & Benbenishty, R. (2014). Gang membership of California middle school students: Behaviors and attitudes as mediators of school violence. *Journal of School Violence*, 13(2), 228–251.

Estrada, J. N., Huerta, A., Hernandez, E., Hernandez, R., & Kim, S. (2018). Socio-ecological risk and protective factors for youth gang involvement. In H. Shapiro (Ed.), *The Wiley handbook on violence in education: forms, factors, and preventions* (pp. 185–202). Hoboken, NJ: John Wiley & Sons.

Fagan, J. (1996). *Gangs, schools and social change*. Lecture given at Teacher College, Columbia University, New York.

Garwood, J. D., Brunsting, N. C., & Fox, L. C. (2014). Improving reading comprehension and fluency outcomes for adolescents with emotional-behavioral disorders: Recent research synthesized. *Remedial and Special Education*, 35(3), 181–194.

Gottfredson, D., Gottfredson, G., & Wiseman, S. (2001). The timing of delinquent behaviors and its implications for after-school programs. *Criminology and Public Policy*, 1(1), 61–86.

Hauth, C., Mastropieri, M., Scruggs, T., & Regan, K. (2013). Can students with emotional and/or behavioral disabilities improve on planning and writing in the content areas of civics and mathematics? *Behavioral Disorders*, 38(3), 154–170.

Huff, C. (1993). Gangs in the United States. In A. P. Goldstein & C. Huff (Eds.), *The gang intervention handbook* (pp. 3–20). Champaign, IL: Research Press.

Jankowski, M. (1991). *Islands in the street: Gangs and American urban society.* Berkeley, CA: University of California Press.

Karcher, C. (1994). *Post-traumatic stress disorder in children as a result of violence: A review of current literature.* Doctoral research paper, Rosemead School of Psychology, Biola University, La Mirada, CA.

Losinski, M., Cuenca-Carlino, Y., Zabocki, M., & Teagarden, J. (2014). Examining the efficacy of self-regulated strategy development for students with emotional or behavioral disorders: A meta-analysis. *Behavioral Disorders*, 40(1), 52–67.

Martorin, A. & Ruiz, P. (2009). Clinical manifestations of psychiatric disorders. In B. Sadock, V. Sadock, & P. Ruiz (Eds.), *Kaplan and Sadock's comprehensive textbook of psychiatry*, 9th ed. (pp. 1071–1107). Baltimore, MD: Lippincott, Williams, & Wilkins.

Miller, W. (1974). American youth gangs: Past and present research. In A. S. Blumberg (Ed.), *Current perspectives on criminal behavior* (pp. 210–239). New York: Knopf.

Nabor, P., May, D., Decker, S., Minor, K., & Wells, J. (2006). Are there gangs in schools? It depends upon whom you ask. *Journal of School Violence*, 5(5), 53–72.

Ralston, Benner, Tsai, Riccomini, & Nelson (2014). Mathematics instruction for students with emotional and behavioural disorders: A best-evidence synthesis. *Preventing School Failure*, 58(1), 1–16.

Sadock, B., Sadock, V., & Ruiz, P. (2009). *Kaplan and Sadock's comprehensive textbook of psychiatry.* Philadelphia, PA: Lippincott Williams & Wilkins.

Taylor, C. (1990). *Dangerous society.* East Lansing, MI: Michigan State University Press.

Thrasher, F. (1927). *The gangs.* Chicago, IL: University of Chicago Press.

Udwin, O. (1993). Annotation: Children's reactions to traumatic events. *Journal of Child Psychology and Psychiatry*, 34(2), 115–127.

Wilkinson, A. (2018, January 23). Why is the World Health Organization issuing a warning about "gaming disorder"? *Second Nexus: Internet Posting*, pp. 1–2.

Young-Pelton, C. A. & Bushman, S. L. (2015). Using video self-modelling to increase active learning responses during small-group reading instruction for primary school pupils with social emotional and mental health difficulties. *Emotional and Behavioural Difficulties*, 20(3), 277–288.

# EPILOGUE

The learning outcomes and social context in local schools are the harbingers and progenitors for the quality of life in the local community. High-performing elementary and secondary schools prepare students with the academic and social competence, attributes and values that are foundational for active participation in a civil and democratic society and for higher educational attainment, occupations and professions with higher income levels, high-quality decision-making, and leadership skills that benefit families and the community. High-performing elementary and secondary schools shape the future for the communities they serve through the quality of preparation provided for the young.

The future of economically and socially distressed communities is especially dependent on the quality of education provided by local schools and on every teacher using highly effective pedagogical practices for students that promote the best interest of the community. The quality of education children receive influences their ability to provide for themselves and their families as adults, their income, access to healthcare, and their life quality and longevity.

The discussion in this book presents powerful pedagogy in practice for transforming urban schools and communities, responding to the various life conditions and needs of children and youth, and supporting every learner in attaining her or his highest potential academically, socially, and psychologically. Powerful pedagogy in practice is grounded in deep knowledge of the learner, the learner's heritage, the community in which the learner lives, and special challenges and circumstances the learner faces in daily life within and outside of school.

Knowing learners includes understanding the relationship between their cultural and experiential background and research and theory on child and adolescent growth and development, knowledge of the indicators for psychological and mental conditions displayed in specific behaviors, and knowing when to consult other professionals for support. Teachers engaged in powerful pedagogy use specific techniques and tools to acquire knowledge about learners, including a *Student Development Inventory* and a *Student Observation Inventory*. Deep knowledge of the learner is the foundation for framing the curriculum, designing meaningful and productive learning experiences, and a supportive social context for learning.

Framing the curriculum to provide access to meaningful learning includes addressing national, state, and local standards; the needs of the local community; the content, structure, and practices in specific disciplines; linking subject matter to learners' cultural heritage, personal experiences, and values; and specific needs for academic, social, and psychological growth and development. The curriculum is designed such that learners understand the application of new knowledge in their everyday lives in the present and the future. Students learn how the knowledge in the school curriculum is used in various occupations and professions. Embedded across the curriculum and grade levels is knowledge that supports students in identifying their role as productive and contributing citizens in the local community, state, and nation.

Powerful pedagogy in practice provides learning experiences that support learners' development academically, socially, and psychologically. Academic learning experiences make connections among new knowledge, ancestral and cultural knowledge, and what students know and have personally experienced. Learning experiences support students in understanding how to apply new knowledge in the present and the future, as well as how to create new knowledge. Further, academic knowledge is used to interpret and propose solutions for issues and questions in the local community.

Teachers using powerful pedagogy in practice provide opportunities for learners' social development that foster feelings of acceptance, belongingness and connectedness through teaching specific attributes and values, essential social skills, and self-regulation. Teachers balance guidance, support, and opportunities through social arrangements in the classroom and specific pedagogical practices that support personal development such as the learner's weekly self-management plan. Teachers address the specific peer-related social needs of children living with stressful situations such as homelessness, foster care, and court affiliation.

Many children and youth have behavioral, mental, and psychological conditions that require special attention, observation, and referral to a licensed professional for examination and potential intervention. The most common among these conditions are depression, post-traumatic stress disorder, toxic stress, trauma, and gang affiliation. In school, children and youth are often punished for displaying behaviors associated with these conditions, rather than being referred to a licensed professional for evaluation and support. In some cases, leaving these conditions untreated or administering punishment leads to long-term and possibly permanent academic, cognitive, and psychological impairment. The discussion in this book describes behavioral indicators for these conditions, observations and documentation that teachers can provide for licensed professionals, and teaching practices that support children and youth affected by these conditions.

Finally, *teaching to transform urban schools and communities* through powerful pedagogy in practice presents a pathway forward for ensuring that every child living in the inner city has access to opportunities for achieving her or his highest potential academically, socially, and psychologically. Those who teach to transform urban schools and communities influence the quality of life for every person living in the inner city.

# INDEX

Note: References in *italics* are to figures, those in **bold** to tables.